PENGUIN BOOKS

THE FAULKNER-COWLEY FILE

William Faulkner was born in New Albany, Mississippi, in 1897 and grew up in Oxford, seat of the University of Mississippi. During World War I he joined the Canadian Royal Flying Corps, but the war ended before his training was complete, and he returned to Oxford to study, briefly, at the university. His first book, a collection of poems entitled *The Marble Faun,* appeared in 1924. *Sartoris* (1929) was his first novel about Yoknapatawpha County, a mythical place that was gradually to become an enormous metaphor not only for the whole of Southern society but also, in many respects, for the world itself. Among other Yoknapatawpha books are *The Sound and the Fury* (1929), *As I Lay Dying* (1930), *Light in August* (1932), *Absalom, Absalom!* (1936), *Go Down, Moses* (1942), and *Requiem for a Nun* (1951), all revolutionary achievements in fictional technique. In 1950 Faulkner belatedly received the 1949 Nobel Prize for Literature. He died in Memphis in 1962.

Born in 1898, Malcolm Cowley grew up in Pennsylvania. He was graduated from Harvard in 1920 and then, in Paris, joined the expatriate American writers, whom he studied in his most famous book, *Exile's Return* (1934; revised 1951). *After the Genteel Tradition: American Writers Since 1910* (1937) and *The Literary Situation* (1954) confirmed his reputation as an outstanding critic, and *Blue Juniata* (1929) and *Dry Season* (1941) brought him recognition as an important modern poet. His most recent book is *A Second Flowering: Works and Days of the Lost Generation* (1973).

The FAULKNER-COWLEY FILE

Letters and Memories, 1944-1962

MALCOLM COWLEY

PENGUIN BOOKS

Penguin Books Ltd, Harmondsworth,
Middlesex, England
Penguin Books, 625 Madison Avenue,
New York, New York 10022, U.S.A.
Penguin Books Australia Ltd, Ringwood,
Victoria, Australia
Penguin Books Canada Limited, 2801 John Street,
Markham, Ontario, Canada L3R 1B4
Penguin Books (N.Z.) Ltd, 182–190 Wairau Road,
Auckland 10, New Zealand

First published in the United States of America by
The Viking Press 1966
First published in Great Britain by
Chatto & Windus Ltd 1967
Viking Compass Edition published 1968
Published in Penguin Books 1978

LIBRARY OF CONGRESS CATALOGING IN PUBLICATION DATA
Cowley, Malcolm, 1898–
The Faulkner-Cowley file.

Reprint of the 1966 ed. published by The Viking Press,
New York.

1. Faulkner, William, 1897–1962. 2. Faulkner,
William, 1897–1962—Correspondence. 3. Cowley, Malcolm,
1898– —Correspondence. 4. Authors, American—20th
century—Biography. I. Faulkner, William, 1897–1962.
II. Title.
[PS3511.A86Z77 1978]   813'.5'2 [B]   77-23751
ISBN 0 14 00.4684 4

Printed in the United States of America by
Offset Paperback Mfrs., Inc., Dallas, Pennsylvania

The speeches on pages 145-46 and 149-50 are copyright © 1958 and 1963, re-
spectively, by Estelle Faulkner and Jill Faulkner Summers. Reprinted by permis-
sion of Random House, Inc., from *Essays, Speeches and Public Letters By William
Faulkner* (James B. Meriwether, ed.). The early draft of "On Privacy—The
American Dream" (pages 132-37) is copyright © 1955 by William Faulkner.
Reprinted by permission of the Estate of William Faulkner and Random House,
Inc. The final draft appears in *Essays, Speeches and Public Letters By William
Faulkner* (James B. Meriwether, ed.).

A NOTE ON SOURCES

Almost all my Faulkner correspondence was given to Yale University, where it is now in the Beinecke Library. I have to thank Mr. Donald C. Gallup, curator of the American collection at Beinecke, for providing me with photocopies. These have been reproduced textually (and orthographically) except for a very few omissions, perhaps a dozen sentences, marked by ellipses. The original letters can be consulted at Beinecke by qualified scholars. Still in my files, by exception, is Faulkner's letter of 16 July, with my answer of July 20, 1948.

The first draft of Faulkner's article "On Privacy—the American Dream: what happened to it" is the property of Mrs. Saxe Commins, who has placed it on deposit with other papers at the Princeton University Library. I am very grateful for her permission to copy it here. The letters to Marshall A. Best and Robert N. Linscott are either in my files or, in some cases, in those of the Viking Press. The letters on Academy business in the next-to-last chapter are from the files of the American Academy of Arts and Letters.

M. C.

The FAULKNER-COWLEY FILE

Almost every critic dreams of discovering some great work that has been neglected by other critics. Some day might he come upon an author whose reputation is less than his achievement and in fact is scandalously out of proportion with it, so that other voices will be added to the critic's voice, in a swelling chorus, as soon as he has made the discovery? That is the dream.

At least once in my critical career I had the good luck to find it realized.

But let me explain that I was by no means the first to discover William Faulkner. The man who most deserves that credit is a lawyer in Oxford, Mississippi, an older friend, Phil Stone, who knew him almost from boyhood, who praised his beginning poems, gave him books to read, and had his secretary type out the early Faulkner stories, until a drawer in his filing cabinet was full of them. Later there was Sherwood Anderson in New Orleans, who walked with Faulkner on many afternoons, drank with him at night, then promised—and kept the promise—to get his first novel published by Horace Liveright if he, Sherwood, didn't have to read the manuscript.

Still later there was Ben Wasson, a Mississippian in New York, who volunteered to act as Faulkner's literary agent. There was Harrison Smith, who served as his editor at

Harcourt, Brace and Company, already a second publisher for the young novelist. Harcourt accepted *Sartoris,* his third book, which had a disappointing sale, then rejected *The Sound and the Fury.* By that time Hal Smith had resigned from Harcourt and had founded a small publishing house of his own. One morning his editorial reader, Lenore Marshall, came running downstairs to say, breathlessly, "I think I have found a work of genius."

Hal must have suspected that it was *The Sound and the Fury,* since he had heard about the book—he may even have read it—while he was still with Harcourt. But he only said, according to Mrs. Marshall, "What's it about?"

"I don't know," she confessed. "I'm just starting it."

"Finish it."

She did, that day, and thereupon reported that *The Sound and the Fury* was indeed a work of genius, though she still didn't know what it was about. The new firm accepted it. On its appearance in 1929, the book had a number of enthusiastic reviews along with the puzzled ones, and it also had enough readers to carry it, after two years, into an extremely modest third printing.

When trying to list the discoverers of William Faulkner, one must mention still other names. There was the late Saxe Commins, his faithful friend and editor at Random House —for the novelist had come to a fourth publisher after Hal Smith's firm went out of business in the depression years.[1] There were the English novelists Arnold Bennett (who said

---

[1] Or rather to a fifth publisher, if one counts the successor firm of Harrison Smith and Robert Haas, which was merged with Random House in 1936. Haas was another good friend of Faulkner's.

he wrote "like an angel") and Richard Hughes; there was the French novelist André Malraux; there was the American novelist Evelyn Scott, joined later by Kay Boyle, and the poet Conrad Aiken. There was in fact a small chorus of admirers, almost wholly composed of creative writers, and it was owing to their support that Faulkner was elected to the National Institute of Arts and Letters in 1939. By that time, however, their voices were almost drowned out by a larger chorus of academic critics, almost all contemptuous, and by a deafening frogpond croak of daily and weekly reviewers. The public, which had been briefly excited by *Sanctuary* in 1931, had ceased to read Faulkner's work.

Consider what might be called his quoted value on the literary stock exchange. By the later years of World War II he had published two books of poems, eleven novels— each an extraordinary work in its particular fashion—two collections of stories, and two cycles of stories, *The Unvanquished* and *Go Down, Moses,* representatives of a hybrid form between the random collection and the unified novel; there were seventeen books in all. In eleven of the books he had created a mythical county in northern Mississippi and had told its story from Indian days to what he regarded as the morally disastrous present; it was a sustained work of the imagination such as no other American writer had attempted. Apparently no one knew that Faulkner had attempted it. His seventeen books were effectively out of print and seemed likely to remain in that condition, since there was no public demand for them. How could one speak of Faulkner's value on the literary stock exchange? In 1944 his name wasn't even listed there.

It was scarcely listed in the immense catalogue of the
New York Public Library, where, at the time, there were
cards for only two of his books, *A Green Bough* and *The
Hamlet*. The other fifteen were hard to find in the second-
hand bookstores on Fourth Avenue. But I had the good
fortune to own many of the books, since I had reviewed
them in *The New Republic* as they appeared. Gradually and
with errors in judgment I was beginning to perceive a pattern that lay behind them.

I had some leisure in the early months of 1944, owing to
a generous grant from the late Mrs. Mary Mellon. I determined to write a long essay on Faulkner and to see whether
it mightn't help to redress the balance between his worth
and his reputation. But first I sent a letter to the author,
addressed to Oxford, Mississippi; it said that I wanted to
meet him and ask questions about his life and his aims.
Three months went by before I received an answer, in an
envelope that bore the address of the Warner Brothers'
studio in Burbank, California.

Hollywood, Sunday, 7 May [1944]

Dear Mr. Cowley:

I just found your letter of last Feb. by idle chance today.
Please excuse this. During the last several years my correspondence has assumed a tone a divination of which
your letter implies. My mail consists of two sorts: from
people who dont write, asking me for something, usually
money, which being a serious writer trying to be an artist,
I naturally dont have; and from people who do write

telling me I cant. So, since I have already agreed to answer No to the first and All right to the second, I open the envelopes to get the return postage stamps (if any) and dump the letters into a desk drawer, to be read when (usually twice a year) the drawer overflows.

I would like very much to have the piece done. I think (at 46) that I have worked too hard at my (elected or doomed, I don't know which) trade, with pride but I believe not vanity, with plenty of ego but with humility too (being a poet, of course I give no fart for glory) to leave no better mark on this our pointless chronicle than I seem to be about to leave.

As you can see from the above, I am at the salt mines again. It would cost more to come here than to come to Miss. This town is crowded with war factory workers and troops, is unpleasant. But I have a cubbyhole which you are welcome to share until June 1, when my family is coming out. In the fall I will go back home. I don't know when I will come East, I mean to New York. I would like to, but I never seem to have that much money anymore, as I try to save what I earn here to stay at home as long as possible on.

I would like the piece, except the biography part. You are welcome to it privately, of course. But I think that if what one has thought and hoped and endeavored and failed at is not enough, if it must be explained and excused by what he has experienced, done or suffered, while he was not being an artist, then he and the one making the evaluation have both failed.

Thank you for your letter, and again excuse the time lapse.

William Faulkner

By the time Faulkner's letter arrived, I was editing a *Portable Hemingway* for the Viking Press. I was late with my copy, the presses were waiting, the Vikings were sending telegrams, and I half expected to find a shipload of berserk warriors moored in front of my door. It wasn't until the job was finished and the threat of sanctions lifted that I wrote Faulkner again.

RFD Gaylordsville, Conn.,
July 22, 1944.

Dear Faulkner:

You can see that I'm pretty nearly as bad as you are about answering letters, and I haven't the excuse of a system either; it's just a mixture of indolence and busyness, one part of each, and life as a succession of deadlines that I just fail to meet.

I want very much to write the article about you, and I want to meet you too, but it's quite possible to write the article without meeting you and without knowing very much about your biography, which wouldn't go into the article anyway—you're right about that point; but I ought to know something about it for the thinking that has to be done before the article is written, so that I wouldn't make too many bad guesses. I'd like to put in about a month or six weeks of work on it, and that's why I'm trying to sell it in advance to some magazine that would pay me for my time; and later I could use it in a book I'm planning to do.

Status of the magazine negotiations: I tried the Atlantic

while I was in Boston, and the net result was a luncheon
at the St. Botolph Club, lobster, sherry, old fashioneds,
two bottles of Bordeaux and some very old rum. The
Atlantic turned thumbs down (thumbs a little greasy with
lobster dipped in butter), first because, I gathered, they had
done something about you some years ago (I didn't read it)[2]
and second because the associate editor seems to be sour on
your work. Now I'm working on Harper's, no luncheon
this time, but Katherine Gauss [Jackson] likes your books
(without knowing much about them) and she was trying
to get a piece I had done on Hemingway, which would
have been turned down by Fred Allen, the chief editor,
so I didn't bother to give it to her—but anyhow that was
an excuse to say that I wanted to do a piece on Faulkner
instead. I'm waiting to hear the verdict. [It was negative.]

Do you want to hear a New York market report on your
standing as a literary figure?

It's about what I suggested in my other letter—very funny,
and a great credit to you, but bad for your pocketbook.
First, in publishing circles your name is mud. They are all
convinced that your books won't ever sell, and it's a pity,
isn't it? they say, with a sort of pleased look on their faces.
(I haven't talked to [Bennett] Cerf [of Random House]
or his new editor, Bob Linscott, about you; but I'm going
to try Linscott, who really likes books, and see whether
I can't get him to do a better job on your next one; if he's
vague or regretful, I should advise your getting another

---

[2] It was Conrad Aiken's fine essay "William Faulkner: The Novel as
Form" (*Atlantic Monthly,* 164, November 1939).

publisher, but I have no idea who he would be.)[3] The bright boys among the critics did a swell job of incomprehending and unselling you, Fadiman especially. Now, when you talk to writers instead of publishers or publishers' pet critics about the *oeuvre* of William Faulkner, it's quite a different story; there you hear almost nothing but admiration, and the better the writer the greater the admiration is likely to be. Conrad Aiken, for example, puts you at the top of the heap. The funny thing is the academic and near-academic critics and the way they misunderstand and misstate your work. You probably haven't read Maxwell Geismar's book, "Writers in Crisis," but he's not so dumb for a professor[4] and does a very good job on Hemingway, but when he comes to Faulkner, you might as well have written your novels in Minoan or Hittite for all the sense he makes of them.

So, a good piece on your work has to be written, and if my indolence doesn't get the best of me, I'll try hard to write it—and thank God, I'm too indolent to stop working once I get started.

Now, there's one question I wish to God you'd answer for me, not because I want to quote you, but so that I won't make a fool of myself when I come to write the piece. It's about the symbolism in your work. It's there, all right, and I don't see how anybody but a learned critic

---

[3] But I thought in a distant way of Scribner's, since I felt (and feel) that Max Perkins was a great editor. Not long afterward I talked to Max about Faulkner; he was not interested. "Faulkner is finished," he said unemphatically.

[4] Geismar is not a professor.

can miss it—I mean, of course, that Sutpen's Hundred, in "Absalom, Absalom!," becomes, for the reader at least, a symbol of the old South, with the manner of its building and its decay after the war, and its owner killed by a poor white, and the only survivor of the Sutpen family a mulatto; that's almost an allegory or legend, and you repeat the legend explicitly in the fourth part of "The Bear."

Once in the Southern Review, Cleanth Brooks, I think it was,[5] gave a whole allegorical scheme for "Sanctuary," saying that the gal was the South, raped by modern industry (in the form of Popeye), except that modern industrial civilization is so sterile it didn't have strength to rape her and had to get a substitute. I thought that Brooks's scheme was a lot too definite and pat, but still Popeye does seem to have something of the quality you impute to the representatives of modern civilization, and the sterility pops up again in the reporter in "Pylon"—and that same book has the sex in the airplane, a marvelous scene with no *double entendre* but with a double meaning, certainly. Well, the question is (speaking roughly) how much of the symbolism is intentional, deliberate? Or is that the sort of question I shouldn't ask, even for my own information?

(I found out when rereading Hemingway that there's a lot of symbolism in his work too, but the question of

---

[5] More errors on my part. Of course the critic was George Marion O'Donnell, who had been the first to recognize that Faulkner was a moralist, and his essay had been published in the *Kenyon Review* (1, Summer 1939), not in the *Southern Review*. Cleanth Brooks's compendious and level-headed study of Faulkner's work had not been started at the time, and would not be published for twenty years.

deliberateness didn't arise there; because the early symbolism was plainly unconscious, and some of the later symbolism—as in "The Snows of Kilimanjaro"—was plainly conscious; in either case the reader wasn't left in much doubt.)

Too much for one letter already. For God's sake don't throw it in the drawer till the drawer gets full.

Sincerely,

Malcolm Cowley

Thanks a lot for the invitation to Hollywood, but I couldn't ever get out there. There's just a chance that I might be able to make a short trip south in the fall, after you get back.—M.

It was a matter of four months before Faulkner answered my query. In the meantime I had been rereading his books, I had assembled a mass of notes on them, and I had started work on an essay that was becoming much longer than I had intended to make it. Two other things I did were to have some bearing on his next letter. First, I had copied out a section of the still unfinished essay and had persuaded the *New York Times Book Review* to publish it. The process made me think of sawing off a steak or a roast from a frozen quarter of beef. Second, I had written to Faulkner repeating my question about his symbolism. To make the question more explicit, I quoted from my essay a paragraph that read:

The reader cannot help wondering why this somber and, at

moments, plainly incredible story [told in *Absalom, Absalom!*] had so seized upon Quentin's mind that he trembled with excitement when telling it and felt that it revealed the essence of the Deep South. It seems to belong in the realm of Gothic romances, with Sutpen's Hundred taking the place of the haunted castle on the Rhine, with Colonel Sutpen as Faust and Charles Bon as Manfred. Then slowly it dawns on you that most of the characters and incidents have a double meaning; that besides their place in the story, they also serve as symbols or metaphors with a general application. Sutpen's great design, the land he stole from the Indians, the French architect who built his house with the aid of wild Negroes from the jungle, the woman of mixed blood whom he married and disowned, the unacknowledged son who ruined him, the poor white whom he wronged and who killed him in anger, the final destruction of the mansion like the downfall of a social order: all these might belong to a tragic fable of Southern history. With a little cleverness, the whole novel might be explained as a connected and logical allegory, but this, I think, would be going far beyond the author's intention. First of all he was writing a story, and one that affected him deeply, but he was also brooding over a social situation. More or less unconsciously, the incidents in the story came to represent the forces and elements in the social situation, since the mind naturally works in terms of symbols and parallels. In Faulkner's case, this form of parallelism is not confined to *Absalom, Absalom!* It can be found in the whole fictional framework that he has been elaborating in novel after novel, until his work has become a myth or legend of the South.

Did that make sense? I asked him. This time Faulkner answered my question at length.

Oxford. Saturday.
[Early November, 1944]
Dear Maitre:

I saw the piece in the Times Book R[eview]. It was all
right. If that is a fair sample, I dont think I need to see
the rest of it before publication because I might want to
collaborate and you're doing all right. But if you want
comments from me before you release it, that's another
horse. So I'll leave it to you whether I see it beforehand
or not.

Vide the paragraph you quoted: As regards any specific
book, I'm trying primarily to tell a story, in the most
effective way I can think of, the most moving, the most
exhaustive. But I think even that is incidental to what I am
trying to do, taking my output (the course of it) as a
whole. I am telling the same story over and over, which
is myself and the world. Tom Wolfe was trying to say everything, the world plus 'I' or filtered through 'I' or the effort
of 'I' to embrace the world in which he was born and walked
a little while and then lay down again, into one volume.
I am trying to go a step further. This I think accounts for
what people call the obscurity, the involved formless
'style', endless sentences. I'm trying to say it all in one
sentence, between one Cap and one period. I'm still trying
to put it all, if possible, on one pinhead. I don't know how
to do it. All I know to do is to keep on trying in a new
way. I'm inclined to think that my material, the South, is
not very important to me. I just happen to know it,
and dont have time in one life to learn another one and

write at the same time. Though the one I know is probably as good as another, life is a phenomenon but not a novelty, the same frantic steeplechase toward nothing everywhere and man stinks the same stink no matter where in time.

Your divination (vide paragraph) is correct. I didn't intend it, but afterward I dimly saw myself what you put into words. I think though you went a step further than I (unconsciously, I repeat) intended. I think Quentin, not Faulkner, is the correct yardstick here. I was writing the story, but he not I was brooding over a situation. I mean, I was creating him as a character, as well as Sutpen et al. He [Quentin] grieved and regretted the passing of an order the dispossessor of which he was not tough enough to withstand. But more he grieved the fact (because he hated and feared the portentous symptom) that a man like Sutpen, who to Quentin was trash, origin-less, could not only have dreamed so high but have had the force and strength to have failed so grandly. Quentin probably contemplated Sutpen as the hypersensitive, already self-crucified cadet of an old long-time Republican Philistine house contemplated the ruin of Sampson's portico . . .[6] He grieved and was moved by it but he was still saying 'I told you so' even while he hated himself for saying it.

You are correct; I was first of all (I still think) telling what I thought was a good story, and I believed Quentin could do it better than I in this case. But I accept grate-fully all your implications, even though I didn't carry

---

[6] There is nothing omitted here. Faulkner sometimes used the ellipsis for punctuation.

them consciously and simultaneously in the writing
of it. In principle I'd like to think I could have. But I
dont believe it would have been necessary to carry them
or even to have known their analogous derivation, to have
had them in the story. Art is simpler than people think
because there is so little to write about. All the moving
things are eternal in man's history and have been written before, and if a man writes hard enough, sincerely
enough, humbly enough, and with the unalterable determination never never never to be quite satisfied with it,
he will repeat them, because art like poverty takes care
of its own, shares its bread.

I am free of Hollywood for six months, must go back
then for the reason that when I was broke in '42 and
the air force didn't want me again, I had to sign a seven
year contract with Warner to get a job. Re the book offer.[7]
I wrote Harold Ober, who forwarded it to me, that I
would not undertake it right now. I can work at Hollywood 6 months, stay at home 6, am used to it now and
have movie work locked off into another room. I dont
want to undertake a book of the nature suggested
because I'm like the old mare who has been bred and
dropped foals 15-16 times, and she has a feeling that she
has only 3 or 4 more in her, and cant afford to spend
one on something from outside. I am working on something now. Random House has about 70 pages of it. I

[7] A publisher with whom I discussed Faulkner's work had suggested that
he write a nonfiction book, on I don't remember what subject, and I had
passed along the suggestion to Harold Ober, who was Faulkner's literary
agent.

will write them to let you see it, if you would like to. It's not Yoknapatawpha this time, though I explained above that I'm still trying to put all mankind's history in one sentence.

> Thank you for letter,
>
> William Faulkner

My best to Hal Smith when you see him.

Faulkner had given me two hints about his work that I confess to not having developed in the essay I was writing. The first was that what he regarded as his essential subject was not the South or its legend, but rather the human situation, "the same frantic steeplechase toward nothing everywhere." He approached it in terms of Southern material because, as he said, "I just happen to know it, and dont have time in one life to learn another and write at the same time." But he hoped that the material would have more than a regional meaning, and very often—as in his comparison of Sutpen with Samson—he thought back to archetypes not in Southern legend, but in the Bible.

The second hint was that he tried to present characters rather than ideas. In that respect his work reminds me of what Northrop Frye says about Shakespeare's plays: that there is not a passage in them "which cannot be explained entirely in terms of its dramatic function and context . . . nothing which owes its existence to Shakespeare's desire to 'say' something." Faulkner was telling me that he had aimed at a sort of dramatic impersonality not only in *Absalom,*

Absalom! but in all his novels. In the same way that it is Quentin Compson, "not Faulkner," who passes judgment on Colonel Sutpen, it would be Isaac McCaslin, not the author of *Go Down, Moses,* who believes that the Southern land has been cursed by injustice to the Negroes; and later it would be Gavin Stevens, not the author of *Intruder in the Dust,* who speaks for the Southern liberals.

But is this a complete statement of the case?

It seems to me that the relation of the author to these three characters in their role as spokesmen is much more complicated than the statement would lead us to believe. Faulkner created the characters, with the stories—or properly speaking, the fables—in which they are involved, and the fact in itself reveals something about the bent of his mind. Simply because they *were* created—because he had given these characters a life that was independent of his own—their ideas belong in the dramatic or novelistic context. They may or may not be the ideas that Faulkner would express when speaking in his own person. On the other hand, these characters speak with too much eloquence, as compared with others who propound more traditional opinions about the South, for the reader not to conclude that Faulkner is applauding them and lending them many of his own convictions.

I felt in November 1944 that an attempt to discuss the complicated relation between author and characters would carry me far beyond the introductory essay on which I was working. At the time I was more concerned with my question about Faulkner's symbolism, and here I was delighted with his answer. It seemed to me then—it still seems to me

—that the deliberate use of symbols is a dangerous literary device, since the author may let himself be distracted from the primary reality of his characters and situations in his effort to give them secondary or symbolic meanings. I felt that truly effective symbols, like those in Faulkner's novels, were produced almost unconsciously, when the author was so deeply absorbed in his story that he made it larger than life. Faulkner's letter helped to confirm me in this belief, and I went back to work on the essay with renewed enthusiasm.

At this point there is a gap of several months in the correspondence. What hadn't been said in my letters is that I had been urging the Viking Press to publish a *Portable Faulkner* as a sequel to the *Portable Hemingway* that I had finished in July. The proposal elicited some interest, but no enthusiasm. I was told that Faulkner's audience was too limited and his critical standing too dubious to justify such a book; it would have no sale. While arguing the point, I had completed my essay, and I was eager to see it in type. But where? The essay had lengthened to the point where no magazine of general circulation would be willing, at the time, to print the whole of it. Accepting the fact, I did the best I could. I beefed it.

The term is one that I first heard from George Milburn, the author of *Catalogue,* an entertaining first novel about an Oklahoma town. His friends waited for a second novel, but it didn't appear. When I asked him about it, he looked unhappy.

"I was spending the winter on Cape Cod," he said, "and I had the book pretty near finished. Then I wanted a pair of riding boots, so I cut off a chunk of it and sold it to *The New Yorker.* There was a bill I owed at the store, and I cut off another chunk. Whenever I needed cash I sold a piece of that novel. It was like I had a steer hanging in the woodshed and was always cutting off steaks. By the end of the winter, Jesus, I'd beefed the whole novel."

So I beefed the essay and published it in sections, wherever an editor was hungry for words. First there had been the article for the *New York Times Book Review*. Then I chopped out a longer section and sent it to Hal Smith, who was then publisher of the *Saturday Review*. There was a still longer section remaining, on Faulkner's legend of the South, and I sent it to Allen Tate, who was editing the *Sewanee Review*. Allen printed it in his summer number. Then suddenly I had a call from the managing editor of the Viking Press, Marshall Best, who asked me to see him at his office.

"It seems to us," he said, "that Faulkner is receiving a great deal of attention in the magazines."

I modestly agreed.

"Under the circumstances," he went on, "we feel that a *Portable Faulkner* might have a chance to attract readers. How soon could you have the copy ready?"

A few days later I wrote a jubilant letter to Faulkner, who was then serving another sentence in Hollywood.

August 9, 1945.

Dear Faulkner:

It's gone through, there will be a Viking Portable Faulkner, and it seems a very good piece of news to me. . . . It won't be a very big transaction from the financial point of view. The Viking Portables have only a moderate sale —the Hemingway I edited sold about 30,000 copies [in the first year] and they thought that was extra good. But the reason the book pleases me is that it gives me a chance to present your work as a whole, at a time when every one of your books except "Sanctuary"—and I'm not even sure about that—is out of print. The result should be a better sale for your new books and a bayonet prick in the ass of Random House to reprint the others.

And now comes the big question, what to include in the book. It will be 600 pages, or a shade more than 200,000 words. The introduction won't be hard; it will be based on what I have written already (bearing your comments in mind)—but what about the text?

I have an idea for that, and I don't know what you'll think about it. Instead of trying to collect the "best of Faulkner" in 600 pages, I thought of selecting the short and long stories, and passages from novels that are really separate stories, that form part of your Mississippi series—so that the reader will have a picture of Yocknapatawpha county [I misspelled the name in those days] from Indian times down to World War II. That would mean starting with "Red Leaves" or "A Justice" from "These Thirteen" —then on to "Was" for plantation days—then one or two of the chapters from "The Unvanquished" for the Civil War, and maybe "Wash" for Reconstruction—you can see the general idea.

I'd like to include "Spotted Horses" (is there much difference between the magazine version and the chapter in "The Hamlet"?), "The Bear" certainly, "All the Dead Pilots" (that being part of the Sartoris cycle), "That Evening Sun" (anthologized till its bones are picked, like

Nancy's in the ditch, but still part of the Compson story),
"Old Man" (from "The Wild Palms"—it's not Yocknapatawpha, but it's Mississippi), "Delta Autumn" and
a lot more.

The big objection to this scheme is that it has nothing
from "The Sound and the Fury," which is a unit in itself,
and too big a unit for a 600-page book that tries to present
your work as a whole; and nothing from "Absalom,
Absalom" (except "Wash," a story with the same characters).
If I include any complete novel it would have to be "As I
Lay Dying," because it is the shortest of them all; it's not
my favorite. But in spite of this objection, I think that a
better picture of your work as a whole could be given in
this fashion. You know my theory, expressed somewhere
in the essay—that you are at your best on two levels,
either in long stories that can be written in one burst of
energy, like "The Bear" and "Spotted Horses" and "Old
Man," or (and) in the Yocknapatawpha cycle as a whole.
The advantage of a book on the system I have in mind
is that it would give you at both these levels, in the stories
and in the big cycle.

I wish I could see you and talk over the whole business.
Not as a matter of idle curiosity, but for my guidance,
I'd like to know, for example, which pieces in some of
your books ("The Hamlet," for instance) were originally
written as separate stories and later fitted into the longer
novel. I wish you had time to go back over your earlier
work and fix up a few factual discrepancies (I called
attention to some of them in my NY Times piece . . .).
For example, the Indians started out being Choctaws (in

"A Justice") and ended up as Chickasaws, which I think is right. (And compare "A Justice" with "The Bear.") But what to hell, those inconsistencies aren't important—the chief thing is that your Mississippi work hangs together beautifully as a whole—as an entire creation there is nothing like it in American literature.

For God's sake, send me an answer to this, because it will soon be time for me to get to work on the book, and I don't want to plan it in a way that would meet with fundamental objections from you.

Did I tell you what Jean-Paul Sartre said about your work? He's a little man with bad teeth, absolutely the best talker I ever met, not the most eloquent but the most understanding. He's the best of the new French dramatists: one of his plays has been running in Paris for more than a year, and he says that his work is based on qualities he learned from American literature. What he said about you was, "Pour les jeunes en France, Faulkner c'est un dieu." Roll that over on your tongue.

Cordially,

Cowley

Faulkner answered my questions promptly, and in detail.

[Hollywood] Thursday. [August 16, 1945]

Dear Cowley:

The idea is very fine. I wish we could meet too, but that seems impossible now. I will do anything I can from here.

By all means let us make a Golden Book of my apocryphal county. I have thought of spending my old age doing something of that nature: an alphabetical, rambling genealogy of the people, father to son to son.

I would hate to have to choose between Red Leaves and A Justice, also another one called Lo! from Story Mag. several years ago. The line dividing the Chickasaw and Choctaw nations passed near my home; I merely moved a tribe slightly at need, since they were slightly different people in behavior.

Yes, there is difference between magazine and Hamlet 'Spotted Horses.' One is a magazine story, shorter and more economical: it is a story made from several chapters of the hamlet, reduced to their essentials. What is lacking in it is the justice of the peace al fresco trial regarding the damage done.

What about taking the whole 3rd section of SOUND AND FURY? That Jason is the new South too. I mean, he is the one Compson and Sartoris who met Snopes on his own ground and in a fashion held his own. Jason would have chopped up a Georgian Manse and sold it off in shotgun bungalows as quick as any man. But then, this is not enough to waste that much space on, is it? The next best would be the last section, for the sake of the negroes, that woman Dilsey who 'does the best I kin.'

AS I LAY DYING is simple tour de force, though I like it. But in this case it says little that spotted horses and Wash and Old Man would not tell.

THE HAMLET was incepted as a novel. When I began it, it produced Spotted Horses, went no further. About

two years later suddenly I had The HOUND, then JAM-
SHYD'S COURTYARD, mainly because SPOTTED HORSES had
created a character I fell in love with: the itinerant
sewing-machine agent named Suratt. Later a man of
that name turned up at home, so I changed my man
to Ratliff for the reason that my whole town spent
much of its time trying to decide just what living man
I was writing about, the one literary criticism of the town
being 'How in the hell did he remember all that, and when
did that happen anyway?'

Meanwhile my book had created Snopes and his clan,
who produced stories in their saga which are to fall in a
later volume: MULE IN THE YARD, BRASS, etc. This over
about ten years, until one day I decided I had better
start on the first volume or I'd never get any of it down.
So I wrote an induction toward the spotted horse story,
which included BARN BURNING and WASH, which I discovered had no place in that book at all. Spotted horses
became a longer story, picked up the HOUND (rewritten
and much longer and with the character's name changed
from Cotton to Snopes) and went on with JAMSHYD'S
COURTYARD.

The Indians actually were Chickasaws, or they may so
be from now on. RED LEAVES actually were Chickasaws.
A JUSTICE could have been either, the reason for their
being Chocktaws was the connection with New Orleans,
which was more available to Chocktaws, as the map herewith will explain.

At this time the Tallahatchie, running from the Chick-

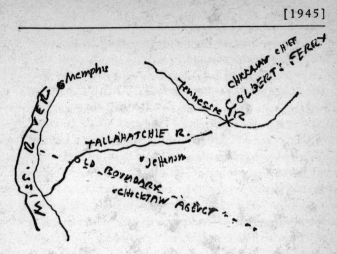

asaw across the Chocktaw nation, was navigable; steam-boats came up it.

Wish to hell we could spend three days together with these books. Write me any way I can help.

Faulkner

Soon I had other problems about "these books," and on September 17 I wrote asking for more advice.

Dear Faulkner:

I finally got down to working on selections for the book, and after the first day I began running into difficulties.

The first day was easy—I simply went back to the stories I remembered with pleasure: "Ad Astra" (with a Sartoris in it), "A Justice," "Red Leaves," "A Rose for Emily" (which has been over-anthologized), "That Evening Sun," "Raid" (from "The Unvanquished"), "Wash" (for the Sutpens), "Old Man," "Was," "The Bear," "Delta Autumn," the chapter from "Light in August" about Warren Grimm —didn't it once come out as a short story?—it was all easy till then, and I had 160,000 words, whereas the book won't hold much more than 200,000. I hadn't started working on "The Hamlet," but my troubles commenced.

Should I use the short-story version of "The Hound" or the somewhat longer version in the novel?

Ditto for "Spotted Horses"?

Ditto for "Barn Burning"—I haven't seen it as a short story, but liked very much the beginning of "The Hamlet," which I suppose it is?

"The Sound and the Fury"—you're probably right about the Jason section being the best one to use separately— the fourth section that follows depends too much on what has gone before, though the Negro sermon and Dilsey over the cold stove saying "I'se seed de first en de last" are wonderful. The trouble with the Jason section for separate use is that without Miss Quentin's running away with the money, it sort of hangs in the air.

"Light in August" I now feel is the best of your novels as novels. I thought when I first read it that it dissolved too much into the three separate stories of Lena Grove (wonderful), Hightower and Joe Christmas—but I read it [again] with the idea that Lena or Joe might be picked

out of the text and found that they were too closely inter-
woven with the others. It would be easy for you to *write*
Joe Christmas into a separate novel, but the anthologist
can't pick him out without leaving bits of his flesh hanging
to Hightower and Lena. So there's nothing to do but take
Warren Grimm, who really comes out all of a piece.

I'll go on mulling over the material, feeling that something very good has to come out of it, because of all
the extraordinary stories that are going into it. That's
one thing about your work—the more one reads it, the
better it seems. It's written, as Gide said of the writing he
liked, to be reread. Did I tell you about the story I heard
from Sartre, about Hemingway drunk in Paris insisting
that Faulkner was better than he was? Hemingway
wrote me a long, rambling, lonely letter complaining
that writing was a lonely trade and there was no one to
talk to about it. He said about you, "Faulkner has the
most talent of anybody but hard to depend on because he
goes on writing after he is tired and seems as though
he never threw away the worthless. I would have been
happy just to have managed him." Hemingway would be
a good manager, too—he knows how to say exactly
what he feels and set a high price on it. But just now he
seems to be very lonely and unhappy . . . and if
you're not corresponding with him already, it would be
nice if you sat down some time and wrote him. His address is

> Finca Vigia
> San Francisco de Paula
> Cuba.

Also it would be wonderful if some time you put your Yocknapatawpha County cycle together yourself—not doing much rewriting, except to make the names agree where you had to change them, but making a lot of cuts in some books. I would say that "Absalom, Absalom" would be better if cut by about a third, maybe all the early parts of it omitted, leaving only Quentin's story to his roommate.

No more today—I don't feel very eloquent; but I should be very grateful for your opinion on the questions I asked toward the beginning of this letter. When I go into New York tomorrow, I'll try to get a list of your stories published in magazines from Harold Ober; there might be things that I ought to include; I still haven't read "Lo!" for example.

As ever,

Cowley

Today I should never assert that *Absalom, Absalom!* "would be better if cut by about a third, maybe all the early parts of it omitted." Also my opinion of *As I Lay Dying* is now much higher than the one expressed in my first letter about the *Portable:* the novel is more than "a simple tour de force," in Faulkner's self-deprecating phrase, and I like it. In 1945 I was still groping for judgments, and my letters often expressed the first that came to mind. I still feel, however, that Faulkner's genius was not primarily novelistic, in the usual sense of the word, but rather epic or bardic. My purpose in 1945 was to reveal that epic quality by emphasizing what others had overlooked: the scope and force and interdependence of his work as a whole.

Faulkner continued to answer my questions in detail.

[Hollywood] Thursday. [September 20, 1945]

Dear Cowley:

Yours of 17th at hand.

If you wish to print 'THE HOUND' and 'SPOTTED HORSES' for the sake of their simple content, use the magazine versions, also 'BARN BURNING' which I think was Harpers, spring 1938 or maybe '39, also in the O HENRY memorial collection, I think they call it, either one of those years or the next, maybe as late as '40. It won a prize, the only damned prize or anything else I ever got for free.

But if you want to use them for their implications of a complete novel (novels) with its (their) particular style, etc., better lift them from the novels, as they were conceived in that form. I like them better in the novel forms, though you have length to watch.

'BARN BURNING' as a story bears the same relation to it as the beginning of 'THE HAMLET' as the other two do to their respective origins. In the mag. 'THE HOUND,' Snopes's name was Cotton. Change it.

Suppose you use the last section, the Dilsey one, of SOUND & FURY, and suppose (if there's time: I am leaving here Monday for Mississippi) I wrote a page or two of synopsis to preface it, a condensation of the first 3 sections, which simply told why and when (and who she was)

and how a 17 year old girl robbed a bureau drawer of
hoarded money and climbed down a drain pipe and ran
off with a carnival pitchman.

Warren Grimm does hold together, whole. If I recall
him aright, he was the Fascist galahad who saved the
white race by murdering Christmas. I invented him in
1931. I didn't realise until after Hitler got into the newspapers that I had created a Nazi before he did.

I'll write to Hemingway. . . .

Faulkner

Will be in Oxford about next Sunday.

It would seem that Faulkner changed his mind. Hemingway made a practice of saving letters, but nothing from
Faulkner was found among his papers.

On October 1 I made a progress report to Marshall Best.

Dear Marshall:

After a lot of rereading and excogitation, I have drawn
up a tentative table of contents for the Faulkner book.
It runs to 248,000 words, but I can squeeze 15,000 words
out of it on demand ("Wedding in the Rain" and "A Rose
for Emily"). It contains no complete novel—though it
does contain one complete story of 47,000 words and
another of 36,000 words. What it offers is a suggestion
of Faulkner's epic, the story of a Mississippi county and

its people from the days when it was inhabited by Chickasaws down to the Second World War, as well as the
long stories in which Faulkner is a master. I think that
for the first time, people will be able to see his talent as
a whole.

All the extracts from novels are stories absolutely independent in themselves (his novels are most of them
composed of stories, which is their greatest structural
fault)—except for the story called "Dilsey," from "The
Sound and the Fury"—and Faulkner has promised to
write me a two-page introduction summarizing the rest
of the novel and making it possible for this story or
episode to stand alone.

Besides the *tentative* table of contents (which I want to
show Faulkner before making it final), there is a list
of the permissions to reprint that must be acquired from
Random House. . . .

About printer's copy, I still lack tear-up copies of "Dr.
Martino," "The Sound and the Fury" and "Sanctuary."
I can get along without them, in a pinch, by sacrificing
my own copies, but it would help me a lot to have them.
One story, "Barn Burning," comes from the June 1939
issue of Harper's Magazine—I haven't that, either, though
it shouldn't be hard to procure. I do have copies of the
other seven books from which I plan to use stories, though
I hate to destroy them. . . .

As ever,

Malcolm

In those days the problem of assembling a printer's manuscript was sometimes a difficult one for anthologists. It was before the time of inexpensive photocopies. Linotypers objected to working from a bound book—they still object—and there was an extra charge if they had to set type from both sides of a printed leaf. Accordingly the anthologist was urged to tear apart two copies of any book from which he was making long extracts. In the case of Faulkner's books, however, even one tear-up copy was hard to find. Viking had advertised in the trade journals and had managed to obtain a few of the books, but nobody came forward with the others. In the end, feeling like Amru at the sack of the Alexandrian library, I had to sacrifice some of my first editions.

Meanwhile I had written Faulkner a letter, now lost, in which I suggested that he might collect his short stories in a volume arranged by cycles: the Indian cycle, the Compson cycle, the town cycle, the Ratliff-Bundren cycle, and all the others. I also told some anecdotes about his reputation in Europe. Again he answered promptly.

[Oxford] Friday. [October 5, 1945]

Dear Cowley:

Yours at hand this morning. I am getting at the synopsis right away, and I will send it along.

The idea about the other volume is pretty fine [that is, the collected stories]. There are some unpublished things which will fit it that I had forgot about, one is another Indian story which Harold Ober has, the agent I mean.

It is the story of how Boon Hogganbeck, in THE BEAR, his
grandfather, how he won his Chickasaw bride from
an Indian suitor by various trials of skill and endurance,
one of which was an eating contest. I forget the title
of it. There is also another Sartoris tale, printed in STORY
two years ago, about Granny Millard and General For-
rest, told by the same Bayard who told THE UNVANQUISHED.
There is an unpublished Gavin Stevens story which
Ober has, about a man who planned to commit a murder
by means of an untameable stallion. You may have seen
these. If you have not, when you are ready to see them,
I will write Ober a note.

Yes, I had become aware of Faulkner's European reputation. The night before I left Hollywood I went (under
pressure) to a party. I was sitting on a sofa with a
drink, suddenly realised I was being pretty intently listened to by three men whom I then realised were squat-
ting on their heels and knees in a kind of circle in
front of me. They were Isherwood, the English poet
and a French surrealist, Hélion; the other one's name I
forget. I'll have to admit though that I felt more like a
decrepit gaffer telling stories than like an old master
producing jewels for three junior co-laborers.

I'll send the synopsis along. It must be right, not just
a list of facts. It should be an induction I think, not
a mere directive.

Faulkner

The induction to the Dilsey section of *The Sound and the Fury* arrived two weeks later in a fat envelope. It was something vastly different from the "page or two of synopsis" that Faulkner had projected in a letter from Hollywood. Instead it was a manuscript of twenty or thirty pages, a genealogy, rich in newly imagined episodes, of the Compson family over a period of almost exactly two centuries, beginning with the battle of Culloden in 1745.

Enclosed with the genealogy was a letter written in the tone of exultation mingled with apology that I have known other writers to adopt after completing a work they felt would stand for a long time. And why the apology? Ostensibly it was offered to me, for the length of the manuscript, but I suspect it was really offered to the fates that had been kind beyond reason, but that still expected him to be humble and submissive, else they would strike him down in his pride.

[Oxford] Thursday. [October 18, 1945]

Cher Maitre:

Here it is. I should have done this when I wrote the book. Then the whole thing would have fallen into pattern like a jigsaw puzzle when the magician's wand touched it.

NOTE: I dont have a copy of TSAF, so if you find discrepancies in chronology (various ages of people, etc) or in the sum of money Quentin stole from her uncle Jason, discrepancies which are too glaring to leave in and which you dont want to correct yourself, send it back to me with a note. As I recall, no definite sum is ever mentioned in the book, and if the book says TP is 12, not 14, you can change that in this appendix.

I think this is all right, it took me about a week to get Hollywood out of my lungs, but I am still writing all right, I believe. The hell of it though, letting me get my hand into it, as was, your material was getting too long; now all you have is still more words. But I think this belongs in your volume. What about dropping DEATH DRAG, if something must be eliminated? That was just a tale, could have happened anywhere, could have been printed as happening anywhere by simply changing the word Jefferson where it occurs, once only I think.

Let me know what you think of this. I think it is really pretty good, to stand as it is, as a piece without implications. Maybe I am just happy that that damned west coast place has not cheapened my soul as much as I probably believed it was going to do.

Faulkner

I may get up east some time this fall. Will let you know.

The completion of that "Appendix," as Faulkner decided to call it, was an event in his career as a novelist. It became an integral part of *The Sound and the Fury* and was the last change he would make in what was to remain his favorite among his own works. Years later he would say, in the extraordinary interview he gave to Jean Stein for the *Paris Review*: [1]

... Since none of my work has met my own standards, I must judge it on the basis of that one which caused me the most grief and anguish, as the mother loves the child who became the thief or murderer more than the one who became the priest.

INTERVIEWER: What work is that?

FAULKNER: *The Sound and the Fury*. I wrote it five separate times, trying to tell the story, to rid myself of the dream which would continue to anguish me until I did. It's a tragedy of two lost women: Caddy and her daughter. Dilsey is one of my own favorite characters, because she is brave, courageous, generous, gentle, and honest. She's much more brave and honest and generous than me.

INTERVIEWER: How did *The Sound and the Fury* begin?

FAULKNER: It began with a mental picture. I didn't realize at the time it was symbolical. The picture was of the muddy seat of a little girl's drawers in a pear tree, where she could see through a window where her grandmother's funeral was taking place and report what was happening to her brothers on the ground below. By the time I explained who they were and what they were doing and how her pants got muddy, I realized it would be impossible to get all of it into a short story and that it would have to be a book. And then I realized the symbolism of the soiled pants, and that image was replaced by the one of the fatherless and motherless girl climbing down the rainpipe to escape from the only home she had, where she had never been offered love or affection or understanding.

I had already begun to tell the story through the eyes of the

---

[1] See *Writers at Work: The* Paris Review *Interviews*, Malcolm Cowley, ed. New York: The Viking Press, 1959.

idiot child, since I felt that it would be more effective as told by someone capable only of knowing what happened, but not why. I saw that I had not told the story that time. I tried to tell it again, the same story through the eyes of another brother. That was still not it. I told it for the third time through the eyes of the third brother. That was still not it. I tried to gather the pieces together and fill in the gaps by making myself the spokesman. It was still not complete, not until fifteen years after the book was published, when I wrote as an appendix to another book the final effort to get the story told and off my mind, so that I myself could have some peace from it. It's the book I feel tenderest towards. I couldn't leave it alone, and I never could tell it right, though I tried hard and would like to try again, though I'd probably fail again.

In this instance Faulkner didn't try again, as he had actually tried in other instances—for example in *Big Woods* (1955), which is partly a recasting of *Go Down, Moses* (1942)—but the truth is that his "Appendix" had brought him closer to success, even by his own impossible standards, than he acknowledged in the interview. After one reads the Compson genealogy, the whole book does fall into pattern "like a jigsaw puzzle when the magician's wand touched it." What seems extraordinary is that he wrote the genealogy sixteen (not fifteen) years after publishing *The Sound and the Fury,* and at a time when he did not own a copy of his favorite novel. Of course he might have found a copy even in Oxford, where his books were not cherished at the time, but he did not feel that he needed to make a search for it. He never set a high value on his printed works, even this one; what possessed him was the story he had tried to tell.

39

The works might disappear from his shelves and even from the second-hand bookstores, but the story lived completely in his mind.

Moreover, it was linked with stories presented in other books, some of which, in that autumn of 1945, were still to be written. The power and persistence of his imagination was (not "were," for power and persistence must be regarded here as related aspects of the same quality) what made him unique among the novelists of his century. Soon I would try, without success, to describe the quality in my introduction to the *Portable*. "All his books in the Yoknapatawpha saga," I would say, "are part of the same living pattern. It is this pattern, and not the printed volumes in which part of it is recorded, that is Faulkner's real achievement. Its existence helps to explain one feature of his work: that each novel, each long or short story, seems to reveal more than it states explicitly and to have a subject bigger than itself. All the separate works are like blocks of marble from the same quarry: they show the veins and faults of the mother rock. Or else—to use a rather strained figure—they are like wooden planks that were cut, not from a log, but from a still living tree. The planks are planed and chiseled into their final shapes, but the tree itself heals over the wound and continues to grow."

III

Like a tree the Compson story had continued to grow, striking roots into the past—as deep as the battle of Culloden—and raising branches into what had been the future when the published novel ended on Easter morning, 1928. That was the morning when it was discovered that Quentin, the younger of Faulkner's "two lost women," had run off with a carnival pitchman after breaking open her Uncle Jason's strongbox— "And so vanished," Faulkner tells us in his Appendix. It is a way of saying that, although she was the last of the Compsons, nothing in her subsequent career had touched his imagination. But the other lost woman, Quentin's mother, he had always regarded with a mixture of horror and unwilling affection. Therefore he follows her to 1943, when she is living in occupied France as a German general's mistress, "ageless and beautiful, cold serene and damned."

It was in this fashion that the story lived in Faulkner's mind, where it grew and changed like every living thing. The more I admired his Appendix, the more I found that some of the changes raised perplexing questions. Where, for example, did Jason keep his strongbox?—under a loose board in the clothes closet, as the novel tells us, or in a locked bureau drawer, as I read in the new manuscript? How much money was in the box?—three thousand dollars, as Jason informed the sheriff in the novel, or nearly seven thousand, as in the Appendix?—where I also learned that $2,840.50 of the larger sum had been saved by Jason himself "in niggard and agonized dimes and quarters and halfdollars"; the novel had implied that all the money in the box was stolen from his niece. How did Quentin escape from Jason's locked room?—did she climb down a pear tree (novel) or slide down a rainspout (Appendix)? Was it Luster or TP (or both) who bounced golf balls against the smokehouse wall, and which of the two Negro boys was older? And what about Jason Compson?—is he altogether repellent and hateful, as in the novel, or should we think of him as having a certain redeeming doggedness and logic, as the Appendix suggests?

Faulkner had challenged me, as it were, to find "discrepancies . . . too glaring to leave in," and it seemed to me that there were more than a few. Also I was worried, in my literalistic fashion, by two French words in the second sentence of his manuscript. They occurred in his account of Ikkemotubbe, the Chickasaw king with whom the first Jason Compson swapped off a race horse for a square mile of land. Faulkner's original manuscript seems to have disappeared, but here, reconstructed from notes, are the first two sentences:

IKKEMOTUBBE. A disposed [sic] American king. Called *du homme* by his fosterbrother, a Chevalier of France, who, had he not been born too late, could have been among the brightest in that glittering galaxy of knightly blackguards who were Napoleon's marshals, who thus translated the Chickasaw title meaning "The Man"; which translation Ikkemotubbe, himself a man of wit and imagination as well as a shrewd judge of character, including his own, carried one step further and anglicised it to 'Doom.'

Of course, I pointed out to Faulkner in a generally enthusiastic letter, the Chevalier of France would have translated Ikkemotubbe's title as *"l'Homme,"* not *"du homme."* I also had some queries about dates—notably for the expulsion of the Chickasaws—and I ended the letter by saying that, since I couldn't undertake to remove the discrepancies, I would shortly return the manuscript for whatever changes Faulkner thought best to make.

He answered immediately.

[Oxford] Saturday. [October 27, 1945]

Dear Cowley:

Letter received. I hope this catches you before you have returned the ms.

I know it's *de l'homme*. I made it incorrect mainly because I decided no one would care especially. That is, it seemed righter to me that Ikke., knowing little of French or English either, should have an easy transition to the apt name he gave himself in English, than that the French should be consistent. Maybe Soeur-Blonde de Vitry deliberately warped his own tongue so Doom could discover his English name. Change it as you see fit.

[I changed it to "Called *l'Homme* (and sometimes *de l'Homme*) by his foster-brother, a Chevalier of France. . . ." Faulkner, whose French was about as good as mine, accepted the emendation.]

43

Jason would call $2840.50 '$3000.00' at any time the sum was owed him. He would have particularised only when *he* owned [owed?] the money. He would have liked to tell the police she stole $15,000.00 from him, but did not dare. He didn't want the money recovered, because then the fact that he had stolen $4000.00 from the thief would have come out. He was simply trying to persuade someone, anyone with the power, to catch her long enough for him to get his hands on her.

(In fact, the purpose of this genealogy is to give a sort of bloodless bibliophile's point of view. I was a sort of Garter King-at-Arms, heatless, not very moved, cleaning up 'Compson' before going on to the next 'C-o' or 'C-r'.)

Re Benjy. This Garter K/A didn't know about the monument and the slipper. He knew only what the town could have told him: a) Benjy was an idiot. B) spent most of his time with a negro nurse in the pasture, until the pasture was deeded in the County Recorder's office as sold. c) was fond of his sister, could always be quieted indoors when placed where he could watch firelight. d) Was gelded by process of law, when and (assumed) why, since the little girl he scared probably made a good story out of it when she got over being scared.

My attitude toward Benjy and Jason has not changed.

Re expulsion of Indians. As I recall I said (approximately) . . . 'the time was 1840 now. . . . and Ikkemotubbe's people were gone from the land too' (Indefinite: implied: might have been last year, 10 years ago, since the preceding established date was within a few years of 1810, or when Jason I rode up Natchez Trace.

Compson domain. . . . etc. etc.

Then you can still date Red Leaves 1845.

I dont say take out DEATH DRAG. I just thought of this to make room for the genealogy. If room for both, leave it.

Faulkner

About Sound & F. Someone at Random House has my copy. About 10 years ago we had notion to reprint, using different color inks to clarify chronology, etc. I underlined my copy in different color crayons, sent it to Bennett [Cerf], never got it back. Will you try telling him you need it? maybe they can dig it up.

Ignorant as I was of heraldic terms, I consulted the *Britannica* and found that the Garter King-of-Arms presides over the Heralds' College, or College of Arms, which rules on questions having to do with armorial bearings and pedigrees. Faulkner had often written as if the author, too, were an imagined character, and the Garter King-of-Arms was his latest avatar. Besides providing him with a fresh approach to the Compson story, his new role had another great advantage. "This Garter K/A," as Faulkner said, ". . . knew only what the town could have told him." Presumably he hadn't read *The Sound and the Fury,* and his ignorance might serve as an excuse for the discrepancies in his narrative.

In that case, however, Faulkner himself was indirectly apologizing for an apparent weakness that was also his strongest quality as a novelist. His creative power was so unflagging that he could not tell a story twice without transforming one detail after another. He waved his magician's wand, and a pear tree in blossom was metamorphosed into a rainspout. He waved the wand again, and four thousand additional dollars appeared in Jason's strongbox, while the box itself, after vanishing from a closet, materialized in a locked bureau drawer. That was easy for him, but I was merely an editor, not a magician, and what was I to say about his text? In retrospect the situation impresses me as a high comedy of misunderstanding. Here was Faulkner striding ahead in his imperial fashion, finding the same sort of excuses for violating the laws of consistency that an emperor finds for invading the realm of a neighboring kinglet; and here was I admiring his boldness, but still mildly objecting that he had told a somewhat different story in the published novel, that the pear tree should still be in blossom, and that Jason was more of a villain than the Appendix made him seem. I can't help feeling that my role was uncomfortably close to that of Polonius or J. Alfred Prufrock:

> No! I am not Prince Hamlet, nor was meant to be;
> Am an attendant lord, one that will do
> To swell a progress, start a scene or two,
> Advise the prince; no doubt, an easy tool,
> Deferential, glad to be of use,
> Politic, cautious, and meticulous;
> Full of high sentence, but a bit obtuse;
> At times, indeed, almost ridiculous—
> Almost, at times, the Fool.

The pedantry and the caution were imposed on me by my role as editor, but I still blame myself for one sort of

obtuseness. I should have realized from the beginning that—
as Faulkner was to tell me in a subsequent letter—the true
Compson story was the one that lived and grew in his imagination. The published book contained only what he had
known about the story in 1929, in other words, only part of
the truth. If I had offered to change everything in the published novel that did not agree with the Appendix, I suspect
that Faulkner would have encouraged me in the under-
taking. It was vastly different, however, when I urged him
to change the Appendix and make it agree with the published book, for that would have meant going back to an
earlier time when he had known or invented much less
about the Compson family.

The discussion was to continue through the winter. Meanwhile, in my role as editorial Polonius or Prufrock, I also
had minor suggestions to make about the text of other passages that were being included in the *Portable*. On November 2 I wrote a long letter to Oxford.

Dear Faulkner:
    This week I've been putting together the printer's
copy of your book. With a single-edged razor blade, I've
been carving out stories and episodes from your other
books, feeling like a vandal in the public library, though
all the copies were my own. I didn't deface "The Sound
and the Fury" because it would be too hard to get another copy. Neither did I write to Bennett Cerf, who
has probably put your copy of TSATF in his private
library as a collector's item. Instead I got a neighbor

who is a good typist to copy out the passage from Part
IV that I'm using, as well as the genealogy of the Compson
family. I expect her to arrive with the manuscript before this letter is finished—then I'll put the carbon
copy of both in a big envelope and mail it to you, so
that you can read the passage from the novel and the new
genealogy together and resolve any discrepancies.

In the other text I have a few changes to suggest, for
this new book where passages from many books are being
printed together, so that the reader will want to know
at the beginning of each story just who is telling it. Here's
a pretty complete list of them:

"A Justice." Since the first sentence of this story will
be the first sentence of the whole book, it ought to name
the people, so I inserted five new words in it, making
it read: "Until Grandfather *Compson* died, we would go
out to the farm every Saturday afternoon. We would leave
home right after dinner in the surrey, I in front with
Roskus, and Grandfather and *Candace* (Caddy, *we
called her*) and Jason in the back." (New words underlined.) It's nice to start the book with a Compson story,
considering that it's going to end with the Compson
genealogy. There's a chronological inconsistency in this
story—it happens, is told, in the year 1900 or thereabouts,
and it deals with the birth of Sam Fathers, who died
in 1885 or 1884—see "The Bear." But I'm not going to
worry about that. Still, you ought to reread the story
for its bearing on the Compson genealogy. I'll have more
to say about that later.

"Wedding in the Rain," being Chapter II of "Absalom,

Absalom." In order to make this piece intelligible by itself, I omitted all the phrases—there was never so much as a whole sentence—that referred to Miss Rosa Cold-field's interview with Quentin in the preceding chapter.— By the way, I had never heard "walked" used in the sense in which it appears in another passage: ". . . even before the coon-hunter Akers claimed to have walked one of them out of the absolute mud like a sleeping alligator and screamed just in time."

"Red Leaves." Is "Three Basket" in this story the same as Herman Basket in "A Justice"? He *could* be the same man, because he's sixty. On Page 158, Had-Two-Fathers couldn't be part of Moketubbe's escort, because he would be twenty-five years old by then and already sold as a slave; so I struck out his name.

"Wash." I changed "His son had been killed in action" to "His son had vanished," to make it agree with the novel.

(Just now the neighbor came with the typescript of TSATF and the Compson genealogy.)

"An Odor of Verbena." Pp. 255-56, I stuck in a couple of past tenses in the story about Sutpen, because now it was 1874 and Sutpen had been scythed down in 1869.

"The Bear." I started the second paragraph, "Isaac McCaslin was sixteen," instead of "He was sixteen," to make it clear from the beginning whom the story is about. In the book, or even published separately in a magazine, that wouldn't be necessary—but here it follows after a story about Bayard Sartoris.— Also, I think Sutpen got his land from Issetibeha, the son, not from Ikkemotubbe, the father. Doom would have been dead in 1833, I think—and on your map in "Absalom, Absalom" you mark the Sutpen land as "Issetibeha's Grant."

"Spotted Horses." The longer version of this story that appeared in "The Hamlet" is infinitely better than the curtailed version in Scribner's, and I am using it, al-fresco trial and all. But it contains one or two short passages intended to tie it up with the rest of the novel, and these I think it would be better to omit. The longest of them is on pages 366 and 367 [of *The Hamlet*]—it's a conversation between Ratliff and Bookwright about Flem Snopes's coming back for Mink Snopes's trial. Nothing to do with the spotted horses. And a paragraph beginning with the last line of p. 367, a speech of Ratliff's about I. O. Snopes, also belongs in the novel but not in this particular story. Which ends, of course, on page 380—"I cant stand no more!" the old Justice cried. "I wont! This court's adjourned! Adjourned!"

"That Evening Sun." I don't suggest any changes. But like some of your other early stories in "These Thirteen," it contains a different chronology from your later novels. Quentin is telling it fifteen years after the events related—yet Quentin had killed himself in 1910. Well, let's not worry about that.

"Old Man." Here's a big question, and you'll have to settle it. Since we're cramped for space, I wonder whether it wouldn't be a good idea to omit the last of the five chapters of this story, and make it end where the convict says, "Yonder's your boat, and here's the woman. But I never did find that bastard on the cottonhouse." When

I took the book apart, it seemed to me that everything that follows is, in a sense, part of the double novel, not part of this particular episode—I mean the convict goes back to the prison farm, while the hero of the other story also goes to prison—that one goes in memory of a woman, the other because he is afraid of women, etc.; the last part of "Old Man" establishes the parallels and contrasts; but the real story ends for me with his surrender to the deputy, and I'd rather put it that way in the book.

"Percy Grimm." The episode starts in the book: "In the town on that day lived a young man named Percy Grimm." For the present book, it would be better to say: "In the town of Jefferson lived a young man named Percy Grimm," so as not to refer to the preceding section. Also, on page 427 of "Light in August" it might be well to add nine words, underlined here: "But when *Joe* Christmas, *the mulatto,* was fetched back from Motts-town on that Saturday afternoon, *accused of killing Miss Joanna Burden* . . ."—so as to make the situation clear. Otherwise the whole episode exists independently.

"Delta Autumn." It might begin: "Soon now they would enter the Delta. The situation was familiar to *old Isaac McCaslin* . . ."—instead of "to him . . ."—so as to make it clear whom the story is about. In "Go Down, Moses" it was perfectly clear; in a magazine it didn't matter.

In the Compson genealogy there are two questions that come up. One of them is a chiefly chronological question about the Indians. Young Ikkemotubbe went down to New Orleans in a keelboat (not many steamboats on

the river then; the first steamboat had appeared in
1808). I noted in another passage that he was still in
New Orleans during the battle in 1815—then he came
back by steamboat; and way up the Tallahatchie River
there was a steamboat ashore that had run there for several
years and then didn't run any more. That would make
1820 about the earliest possible year for his return. But in
the genealogy, you have Jason Lycurgus Compson coming up the Natchez Trace in 1811 and winning a square
mile of land from Ikkemotubbe or Doom just a few
months later.— Either Jason Lycurgus' trip up the trace
should have been made in 1820, which would answer all
questions; or else make it vague about how long he
spent in the Chickasaw Agency before he won the land.

The second question in the genealogy is about the fe-
male Quentin and how she stole the money from her
uncle and how much she stole. You'll have to read the
typed passage from TSATF and settle that question yourself. I ended the passage with "I seed de first en de last,"
according to my original notion, rather than following
Jason to Mottstown and Benjy around the left side of
the monument.

Those are about all my questions. The rest of the
manuscript is all ready now, except for my introduction,
which I'll rewrite from what I've done already—but I
want to hand in your text first, hand it in very quickly,
so I'll be very, very grateful if you can go over this
stuff right away. I'm keeping a carbon of this letter, so
that you won't have to go into so many details in your
answer. Also, of the typescript I have the original, so don't

bother to send me back any pages except those on which you make corrections—that'll save postage, and maybe you can send it air mail. No more now. I think I'm seeing daylight, and I think it's going to be, and not thanks to me, a wonderful book.

As ever,
Cowley

Five days later I received an air-mail envelope from Faulkner. What it contained was two pages of typing without superscription or signature.

I never made a genealogical or chronological chart, perhaps because I knew I would take liberties with both —which I have.

Issetibeha was the chief who conveyed the patent from which all the land sales to the whites derived. He owned the slave who was pursued to complete his suttee.

Moketubbe was his son, the dropsical man in the too-tight shoes, who followed the pursuit of the fleeing slave in a palanquin.

Ikkemotubbe, Doom, was Issetibeha's sister's son, who frightened Moketubbe into abdicating.

Hence RED LEAVES would have to precede A JUSTICE, by actual chronology.

I assume you plan to 'date' by specific year each story as it appears. If you wish to put A JUSTICE first, what about simply leaving the date off RED LEAVES when

it appears? granted that you wish to cover the approxi-
mate decade 1840 plus by so dating Red Leaves. All these
grants (deeds) were recorded before 1840, by which
time this country had become 'white' country, though
a few Chickasaws still retained holdings under the white
man's setup. (the patent for my home is 1833)

Had-Two-Fathers was the son of Doom and the slave
woman in A JUSTICE. Sam Fathers was actually Had-
Two-Fathers' son, and hence the *grandson* of a king.

I realised some time ago you would get into this inconsistency and pitied you. I suggest you make dates, when
you state them, as vague as possible. Say, in these Indian
pieces, when you state a date, call it '18—' or 'ante
1840.'

I think your plan of sequence is the right one. If I were
doing the book, I would keep your plan, simply not
date specifically the pieces, or give them their correct
date regardless. I would date A JUSTICE when it happened, then date RED LEAVES when it happened, regardless of whether it preceded A JUSTICE in time. Or I would
specify a date *only* for each section: like this.

> SECTION 1. THE OLD PEOPLE. 1800-1860.
> "   2. THE UNVANQUISHED. 1860-1874.

I agree with your plan of inserting words to establish
who and when and where, wherever you wish.

'Walked up' is used by any hunter or woodsman in
this country. [But Faulkner had written "walked . . .
out of," and that was what confused me.] The dog 'finds'
the birds, or when the dog fails, the gunner 'walks them

up' by accident or hope. The deer hunter 'walks up' a deer. It means the hunter steals through the woods skilfully enough to get close enough to the game to flush it within shooting range.

THREE BASKET was one of ISSETIBEHA's men (Warriors), probably a minor leader. The country was getting overrun by white men about then. Herman Basket was Three Basket's son, with a halfwhite name, a young blood, a wild companion of young Ikkemotubbe, who became Doom.

Sutpen's deed would derive from Isstibeha's grant, since Issetibeha as the chief granted all the land, that is, made treaty to surrender the patent, though the white purchaser's deed from the govt. might be dated years later. Ikkemotubbe (Doom), as Issetibeha's inheritor, would have sold land still under his uncle's patent.

All right about SPOTTED HORSES.

Dont worry either about chrn. in EVENING SUN.

OLD MAN. By all means. The story ends with: 'Here's your boat' etc. Stop it there.

[But later I would decide, after reading "Old Man" still another time, that I had been wrong to suggest omitting the last chapter, and that Faulkner had been wrong, or needlessly polite, in accepting the suggestion. The story appears in the *Portable* exactly as he wrote it.]

PERCY GRIMM. All right.

DELTA AUTUMN. All right.

Will rewrite portions of the APPENDIX.

Faulkner returned his copy of the retyped Appendix a day or two later, if I remember correctly, with minor corrections that removed some, but not all, of the discrepancies I had mentioned.

He didn't make a practice of saving letters. My next one might have disappeared with several others of which I made no carbon, but this time Faulkner sent it back with comments in the margin written in his small, angular, precise hand.

November 10, 1945.

Dear Faulkner:

Thanks & thanks again for shooting the information back to me. I've got the manuscript pretty well in shape now, and I figure on giving it to the publisher Monday or Tuesday, depending on when I get in to New York. My own text is still to do—it can wait a couple of weeks. It will be a boiling down and rewriting of what I have said already.

In the last few days, thinking it over, I decided on a couple of changes. "Barn Burning" didn't seem as good to me as some of the other stories, and since the book is too long already, I decided to leave it out. "Spotted Horses" can stand for the peasants, being about 24,000 words, and wonderful. Instead of "Ambuscade," the first story in "The Unvanquished," I thought and thought and decided to use "Raid"—for if the book didn't have those black people tramping the roads to Jordan, it wouldn't be the book I want it to be.

[Faulkner wrote in the margin, "Good!!! Would have done so myself to begin with."]

Also I thought and thought and decided that the two-page induction you did for "Go Down, Moses"—it's printed as the first two pages of "Was," but it's about Ike McCaslin, not his cousin Carothers McCaslin Edmonds in the old days —I decided that those two pages might as well come out, because they belong to GDM as a book, not to that particular story. OK?

[Faulkner wrote in the margin, "O.K."]

I decided to let the dates stand with one exception—the date before "Red Leaves" will just be "18—." That was one of your suggestions, and a good one. Actually, in "Red Leaves," Ikkemotubbe, or Doom, is described as the father of Issetibeha, not vice versa. Reread it and see. Some day you *will* have to go over those early stories and change the dates and genealogies to fit with your present plan. Maybe before the collected short stories appear. The book still opens with "A Justice," which is fine and is, moreover, a Compson story.

I made the corrections in the Appendix, and many thanks for them. There are three more I'd suggest, very small ones:

1. Quentin in the novel climbed down a pear tree, not the rain spout. Shouldn't I change this?

[Faulkner wrote in the margin, "Could still be the Garter K/A, whose soul is one inviolable literary cliché. He would insist on 'gutter.'"]

2. On the very last page you say of TP: "Who wore on Memphis' Beal Street the fine bright cheap intransigeant

RFD Gaylordsville, Conn.,
November 10, 1945.

Dear Faulkner:

Thanks & thanks again for shooting the information back to me.
I've got the manuscript pretty well in shape now, and I figure on giving
it to the publisher Monday or Tuesday, depending on when I get in to
New York. My own text is still to do—it can wait a couple of weeks.
It will be a boiling down and rewriting of what I have said already.

In the last few days, thinking it over, I decided on a couple of
changes. "Barn Burning" didn't seem as good to me as some of the other
stories, and since the book is too long already, I decided to leave it
out. "Spotted Horses" can stand for the peasants, being about 24,000
words, and wonderful. Instead of 22nd "Ambuscade," the first story in
"The Unvanquished," I thought and thought and decided to use "Raid"—
for if the book didn't have those black people tramping the roads to
Jordan, it wouldn't be the book I want it to be. Also I thought and
thought and decided that the two-page induction you did for "Go Down,
Moses"—it's printed as the first two pages of "Was," but it's about
Ike McCaslin, not his cousin Carothers McCaslin Edmonds in the old days
—I decided that those two pages might as well come out, because they
belong to GDM as a book, not to that particular story. OK?

[margin right:] good !!!
Would have
done so
myself
to begin
with.

[margin:] O.K.

I decided to let the dates stand with one exception—the date before
"Red Leaves" will just be "18—." That was one of your suggestions, and
a good one. Actually, in "Red Leaves," Ikkemotubbe, or Doom, is described
as the father of Issetibeha, not vice versa. Reread it and see. Some day
you will have to go over those early stories and change the dates and
genealogies to fit with your present plan. Maybe before the collected
short stories appear. The book still opens with "A Justice," which is
fine and is, moreover, a Compson story.

I made the corrections in the Appendix, and many thanks for them.
There are three more I'd suggest, very small ones:

[margin left:] Could still be the
gamble k/A, whme
sad is one invisible
literary cliché. He
would insist on
'gutter'.

1. Quentin in the novel climbed down a pear tree, not the rain
spout. Shouldn't I change this?

[margin left:] all night

2. On the very last page you say of TP: "Who wore on Memphis'
Beal Street the fine bright cheap intransigeant clothes manufactured
specifically for him by the Jew owners of Chicago and New York sweatshops."
In these present days, I'd like to drop out the word "Jew"—people won't
think they're by any chance Arab or Chinese; and with all that's going
on I'd rather not see a false argument over anti-Semitism injected into
the reviews.

[margin left:] All night

3. A phrase that seems to be out of place. The context reads:
". . . only the Negro woman, his sworn enemy since his birth and his
mortal one since that day in 1911 when she too divined by simple clairvoyance that he was somehow using his infant niece's illegitimacy to
blackmail its mother, who cooked the food he ate." End of sentence.
Shouldn't it read ". . . only the Negro woman who cooked the food he
ate, his sworn enemy since his birth and his mortal one since that
day in 1911 . . ." etc.?

#2

The book is getting along to the point where I think it's looking
fine—Godawmighty it's wonderful; and I wonder whether the reviewers
will really _read_ you this time instead of judging by their preconceived
ideas and their memories of what Clifton Pen Fadiman said in the days
when he was writing for the New Yorker. I talked to Bob Linscott about
the idea of printing your collected stories 1 year after the Viking
book appears, and he was all for it. And now, what about that trip to
New York you've been talking about? Do you know where you're going
to stay while there? Would you like me to put you up at the Harvard
Club for two weeks, the only cheap hotel in the Midtown section, and
no stranger talks to you there any more than he would in the Harvard
Yard? Don't come up without having a place to lay your head.

As ever,

Cowley

mentioned in the stories
we're using.

P.S. You remember the map of Yoknapatawpha County printed at the
end of "Absalom, Absalom"? I think it would be a very good idea to
reproduce it in the Viking book if at all possible—or you might even
want to draw a new one, showing the Compson domain and other things.
    "If at all possible," I said, because in a $2 book they can't af-
ford to reproduce the map on a two-page folded insert—it would have to
fit somehow into the regular succession of pages. I'm sending it on
to Marshall Best at Viking to see what he thinks he can do.—MC.

Can Imyn "compum" on the old map - if I had it.

PPS. Three times on first two pages of the
Appendix you use the word "disposessed." I can't
find it in my dictionary. Is it a slip of the
typewriter for "dispossessed"?

Lots of trouble I'm making for you.

M

Yes, damn it.

59

clothes manufactured specifically for him by the Jew owners of Chicago and New York sweatshops." In these present days, I'd like to drop out the word "Jew"—people won't think they're by any chance Arab or Chinese; and with all that's going on I'd rather not see a false argument over anti-Semitism injected into the reviews.

[Faulkner wrote in the margin, "All right."]

3. A phrase that seems to be out of place. The context reads: ". . . only the Negro woman, his sworn enemy since his birth and his mortal one since that day in 1911 when she too divined by simple clairvoyance that he was somehow using his infant niece's illegitimacy to blackmail its mother, *who cooked the food he ate*." End of sentence. Shouldn't it read, ". . . only the Negro woman *who cooked the food he ate,* his sworn enemy since his birth and his mortal one since that day in 1911 . . ." etc.?

[Again Faulkner wrote in the margin, "All right." But later, when revising the Appendix for another book, he restored the sentence to its original form.]

The book is getting along to the point where I think it's looking fine—Godawmighty it's wonderful; and I wonder whether the reviewers will really *read* you this time instead of judging by their preconceived ideas and their memories of what Clifton Fadiman said in the days when he was writing for the New Yorker. I talked to Bob Linscott [of Random House] about the idea of printing your collected stories 1 year after the Viking book appears, and he was all for it. And now, what about that trip to New York you've been thinking about? Do you know where you're going to stay while there? Would you like me to put you

up at the Harvard Club for two weeks, the only cheap
hotel in the Midtown section, and no stranger talks to
you there any more than he would in the Harvard Yard?
Don't come up without a place to lay your head.

As ever,
Cowley

P.S. You remember the map of Yoknapatawpha County
printed at the end of "Absalom, Absalom"? I think it
would be a very good idea to reproduce it in the Viking
book if at all possible—or you might even want to draw
a new one, showing the Compson domain and other
things mentioned in the stories we're using.

"If at all possible," I said, because in a $2 book they can't
afford to reproduce the map on a two-page folded insert
—it would have to fit somehow into the regular succession
of pages. I'm sending it to Marshall Best at Viking to see
what he thinks he can do.—MC.

[Faulkner wrote in the margin, "Can log in 'Compson'
on the old map—if I had it."]

PPS. Three times on first two pages of the Appendix you
use the word "disposessed." I can't find it in my dictionary.
Is it a slip of the typewriter for "dispossessed"?

Lots of trouble I'm making for you.—M

[Faulkner wrote at the foot of the page—with an arrow
pointing to "dispossessed"—"Yes, damn it."]

Even before my questions were answered, I wrote ex-
ultantly to the Viking Press.

November 11, 1945.

Dear Marshall:

The Faulkner text is ready to shoot—I'm hoping to give
it to someone going to New York, so as to avoid the risk
and expense of the mails. My introduction and seven
prefaces are still to write. . . .

I enclose Faulkner's map of Yoknapatawpha County,
printed as a pasted & folded insert in "Absalom, Absalom."
Is there any way to use it in our volume, say on facing
pages? It would have to be relettered and reproduced all
black instead of 2-color. Or, another possibility, I might
persuade Faulkner to draw a new map.

I am very pleased with the volume as it now stands.
Every story in it is (1) complete in itself, no matter how
long or short; and (2) contributes to the history of
Yoknapatawpha County, so that the volume as a whole
is close to being a novel in itself. Other writers are being
rediscovered and revalued. I think it's Faulkner's turn this
year, for he's the best of them.

As ever,
Malcolm

IV

During the next month, while I worked on the introduction, most of my correspondence was concerned with two subjects. One of them was Faulkner's map of Yoknapatawpha County; the other was the descriptive text to be printed on the jacket of the *Portable*. On those two subjects I exchanged a number of letters with the Viking Press.

Marshall Best wrote me about the map on November 20, 1945. "I am sure we can get it in somehow," he said. "If Faulkner would draw a new map it would be an added touch." Then, after consulting with the production department, he added, "Better let us have the lettering done as his is not very legible—especially if it is further reduced to the Portable size. We will use it as an endpaper turned sideways. I am returning the map as you may not have a copy." I promptly forwarded the map to Faulkner.

In the same letter Marshall wrote: "I enclose rough copy for the front of the jacket. Is this what we ought to say and have a right to say?" His rough copy read:

THE PORTABLE FAULKNER
The saga of Yoknapatawpha County, Mississippi
(1820-1945)—in effect, a new work by William Faulkner,
drawn from his best published novels and short stories,
with connective material and notes on the characters
supplied by himself.

I did not think that this was quite what we ought to say, and I exchanged letters with Viking on the subject. In one of them I also went back to the sempiternal question of the pear tree and the rainpipe (or rainspout). "There is one change that I made in pencil on the ms. of his Appendix," I said on November 25, "that it turns out he didn't approve of (he has okayed everything else). The change he didn't like is that he wrote that Quentin, the girl, got into Jason's room by the rain spout. I changed 'rain spout' to 'plum tree' [of course my change had been to "pear tree"; the letter was hastily written], to make it agree with the earlier text of the novel—but Faulkner has a rather involved reason why he would like to have it changed back to 'rain spout' here, while letting 'plum tree' stand in the Dilsey passage of the novel. So, a note for the copy or proof reader—in the Appendix, wherever 'rain spout' is changed to 'plum tree' in pencil, rub out the change—if it's still in ms.—or correct it to 'rain spout' in proof, if it has gone to the printer."

By somebody's oversight—probably mine in reading proof —this final change was never made. In the *Portable* version of the Appendix, Quentin still escapes from Jason's locked room by climbing down a pear tree.

Faulkner's redrawn map reached me early in December, and I sent it on to Marshall Best. "It still needs the attention of a map maker," I told him. "I'm enclosing it with notes of my own, which I think will clear up the doubtful points. . . . I'm having a hard time with the introduction, principally because it was all written a year ago, and now it has gone and frozen on me, so that I have to work like hell to transform it from a general essay into a piece belonging at the front of a Viking Portable."

I had sent Faulkner the proposed jacket copy and had said that I questioned the phrase "—in effect, a new work by William Faulkner." In the same letter I had mildly complained about the lack of biographical details. There was hardly anything in *Who's Who* except the place and date of his birth. (b. New Albany, Miss., Sept. 25, 1897) and the titles of his books. The sketch was followed by an asterisk to signify—in the special language of the editors— "that either the published biography could not be verified, or that at least temporary non-currency in respect to general reference interest has been indicated by lack of change in the data or failure to receive requested information." I translated: Faulkner hadn't been answering letters from *Who's Who*. He was listed there as William Falkner, without a "u." What, I asked, was the proper spelling of his name?

Once again he answered my questions at length.

[Oxford] Saturday. [December 8, 1945]

Dear Cowley:

You should have the map by now.

You are right, the phrase wont do, out of regard to Random House. Could it read something like this:

... saga of ... county ...
A chronological picture of Faulkner's apocryphal
Mississippi county, selected from his published works,
novels and stories, with a heretofore unpublished
genealogy of one of its principal families.
Edited by M. Cowley

It's not a new work by Faulkner. It's a new work by Cowley all right through. If you like, you might say 'the first chronological picture' etc.

The name is 'Falkner'. My great-grandfather, whose name I bear, was a considerable figure in his time and provincial milieu. He was prototype of John Sartoris: raised, organised, paid the expenses of and commanded the 2nd Mississippi Infantry, 1861-2, etc. Was a part of Stonewall Jackson's left at 1st Manassas that afternoon; we have a citation in James Longstreet's longhand as his corps commander after 2nd Manassas. He built the first railroad in our county, wrote a few books, made grand European tour of his time, died in a duel and the county raised a marble effigy which still stands in Tippah County. The place of our origin shows on larger maps: a hamlet named Falkner just below Tennessee line on his railroad.

My first recollection of the name was, no outsider seemed able to pronounce it from reading it, and when he did pronounce it, he always wrote the 'u' into it. So it seemed to me that the whole outside world was trying to change it, and usually did. Maybe when I began to write, even though I thought then I was writing for fun, I secretly was ambitious and did not want to ride on grandfather's coat-tails, and so accepted the 'u', was glad of such an easy way to strike out for myself. I accept either spelling. In Oxford it usually has no 'u' except on a book. The above was always my mother's and father's version of why I put back into it the 'u' which my greatgrandfather, himself always a little impatient of grammar and spelling both, was said to have removed. I myself really dont know the true reason. It just seemed to me that as soon as I got away from Mississippi, I found the 'u' in the word whether I wished it or not. I still think it is of no importance, and either one suits me.

I graduated from grammar school, went two years to highschool, but only during fall to play on the football team, my parents finally caught on, worked about a year as a book-keeper in grandfather's bank, went to RAF, returned home, attended 1 year at University of Mississippi by special dispensation for returned troops, studying European languages, still didn't like school and quit that. Rest of education undirected reading.

The above I still hope can remain private between you and me, the facts are in order and sequence for you to use, to clarify the whos who piece. The following is for your ear too. What I have written is of course in the public domain and the public is welcome; what I ate and did and when and where, is my own business.

I more or less grew up in my father's livery stable. Being the eldest of four boys, I escaped my mother's influence pretty easy, since my father thought it was fine for me to apprentice to the business. I imagine I would have been in the livery stable yet if it hadn't been for motor car.

When I came back from RAF, my father's health was beginning to fail and he had a political job: business manager of the state University, given to him by a countryman whom my grandfather had made a lawyer of, who became governor of Mississippi. I didn't want to go to work; it was by my father's request that I entered the University, which I didn't want to do either. That was in 1920. Since then I have: Painted houses. Served as a 4th class postmaster. Worked for a New Orleans bootlegger. Deck hand in freighters (Atlantic). Hand in a Gulf of Mexico shrimp trawler. Stationary boiler fireman. Barnstormed an aeroplane out of cow pastures. Operated a farm, cotton and feed, breeding and raising mules and cattle. Wrote (or tried) for moving pictures. Oh yes, was a scout master for two years, was fired for moral reasons.[1]

Faulkner

On December 18 I wrote a happy letter to the Viking Press.

Dear Marshall:

Today I finished the Faulkner introduction and sent it off to be retyped, because I wanted carbons of it, one to send to Faulkner and another to send to Allen Tate. About the copy to Allen Tate there hangs a tale. Last spring I gave Allen part of the long Faulkner piece I had done, a part called "William Faulkner's Legend of the South." Allen kept asking me to enter it in an essay contest organized by The Sewanee Review, and finally (before you asked me to do the Portable) I consented. Prize-winning pieces in the contest were to be printed— perhaps—in a book by Prentice-Hall, which was putting up the prize money. Well, my Faulkner piece has won the essay prize of $200. That wasn't such a big joy to me as it

---

[1] That is, because he was the author of *Sanctuary*.

might have been otherwise, because I wanted to use part of that essay in the introduction. As a matter of fact, I *have* used part of that essay in the introduction, about 2,500 of the 6,000 words, with some revisions; and I want to see whether Allen approves of what I have done. . . .

[Allen approved; and Prentice-Hall kindly gave me permission to use the twenty-five hundred words.]

The introduction as it stands is, I think today—don't know what I'll think tomorrow—the best single essay I have ever written. Now I'll go to work on the short editor's prefaces, which won't be so hard.

Faulkner didn't think we should use the phrase, "In effect, a new work by William Faulkner." He said, "The phrase won't do, out of respect to Random House. . . . If you like, you might say, 'The first chronological picture of Faulkner's apocryphal Mississippi county.'"

Well, I mulled over Faulkner's objection and suggestion, and I came up with the following text [which was the one finally used]:

The saga of Yoknapatawpha County, 1820-1945, being the first chronological picture of Faulkner's mythical county in Mississippi—in effect a new work, though selected from his best published novels and stories; with his account of one of the principal families written especially for this volume.

I don't think anybody would have a right to object to "in effect a new work, though selected. . . ."; that's pretty nearly a plain statement of fact.

How's the map coming? And everything else?

As ever,
Malcolm

The map was finished, so I learned, and everything else was coming fine. But I wondered what Faulkner would say after reading the introduction. I hoped he would like it. I believed, though not confidently, that he would like it. And he did like most of it, as I was soon to learn; he even accepted my reservations about his work. I had felt that it was necessary, however, to include a few biographical details, not those he had told me in confidence, but others I had gathered from the sources available in New York. To those details he objected strongly, and they would become the subject of a protracted discussion that had its comic overtones.

V

Among the writers of his time, Faulkner was altogether exceptional in the value that he placed on privacy. It was not that he had a great secret, or more than the usual quota of little secrets; it was simply that he could not bear to have his personal affairs discussed in print. To find anything like his feeling in that respect, one would have to go back to Henry James and the abhorrence for published gossip that he expressed in short novels like *The Reverberator* and *The Papers*. But again like Henry James—though in a fashion of his own—Faulkner had a habit of doing and saying things that made good stories and that proved to be the crack in his armor. The stories were repeated by his friends to strangers and by strangers to newspaper columnists, often with an embroidery of details, until at last they were printed as largely erroneous accounts. These Faulkner seldom read, and apparently he made a principle of never correcting them, with the result that the errors became sanctified by repetition.

In my search for dependable information I had turned to a useful reference work, *Twentieth Century Authors* (1942). It was edited by Stanley J. Kunitz and Howard Haycraft with some concern for accuracy, in a field where legends abound, but the conflicting stories about Faulkner had proved too much for them. For example, their account of his wartime activities is a short paragraph containing—as I afterward learned—at least five misstatements of fact. It reads:

The First World War woke him from this lethargy. Flying caught his imagination, but he refused to enlist with the 'Yankees,' so went to Toronto and joined the Canadian Air Force, becoming a lieutenant in the R.A.F. Biographers who say he got no nearer France than Toronto are mistaken. He was sent to France as an observer, had two planes shot down under him, was wounded in the second shooting, and did not return to Oxford until after the Armistice.

I wanted to accept that paragraph because I had come to think of Faulkner, perhaps rightly, as being among the "wounded writers" of his generation, with Hemingway and others. It was hard for me to believe that his vivid stories about aviators in France—"Ad Astra," "Turnabout," "All the Dead Pilots"—and his portraits of spiritually maimed veterans, living corpses, in *Soldier's Pay* and *Sartoris* were based on anything but direct experience. At the same time I wanted to follow his wishes by giving no more than the necessary bare details of his life. So I had mentioned his wartime adventures at the very beginning of my introduction, but had disposed of them in only three sentences:

When the war was over—the other war—William Faulkner went back to Oxford, Mississippi. He had been trained as a flyer in Canada, had served at the front in the Royal Air Force, and, after his plane was damaged in combat, had crashed it behind the British lines. Now he was home again and not at home, or at least not able to accept the postwar world.

What I did not realize was that my second sentence, rewritten as it was from the paragraph in *Twentieth Century Authors,* included three of the misstatements. There was nothing right in it except that Faulkner had been trained as a flyer in Canada. Still, I did not dream that my facts were wrong or that Faulkner would question them. I was worried, however, by some reservations I had offered on a later page about his prose style. I had conjectured that its faults were due partly to his always having worked in solitude. In this connection I had quoted some remarks made by Henry James in his little book about Hawthorne. "Great things," James says, "have of course been done by solitary workers; but they have usually been done with double the pains they would have cost if they had been produced in more genial circumstances. The solitary worker loses the profit of example and discussion; he is apt to make awkward experiments; he is in the nature of the case more or less of an empiric. The empiric may, as I say, be treated by the world as an expert; but the drawbacks and discomforts of empiricism remain to him and are in fact increased by the suspicion that is mingled with his gratitude, of a want in the public taste of a sense of the proportion of things." After quoting from James, I had continued:

Like Hawthorne, Faulkner is a solitary worker by choice, and he has done great things not only with double the pains to himself that they might have cost if produced in more genial circumstances, but sometimes also with double the pains to the reader. Two or three of his books as a whole and many of them in part are awkward experiments. All of them are full of over-blown words like "imponderable," "immortal," "immutable," and "immemorial" that he would have used with more discretion, or not at all, if he had followed Hemingway's example and served an apprenticeship to an older writer. He is a most uncertain judge of his own work, and he has no reason to believe that the world's judgment is any more to be trusted; indeed, there is no American writer who would be justified in feeling more suspicion of "a want in the public taste of a sense of the proportion of things."

What would Faulkner say about my strictures?—In his first letter after reading the introduction, he said nothing at all about them, though later he was to discuss them briefly. He perturbed me, however, by objecting to my mention of his wartime experiences.

[Oxford] Monday. [December 24, 1945]

Dear Cowley

The piece received, and is all right. I still wish you could lead off this way:

When the war was over—the other war—William Faulkner, at home again in Oxford, Mississippi, yet at the same time was not at home, or at least not able to accept the postwar world.

Then go on from there. The piece is good, thoughtful, and sound. I myself would have said here:

'or rather what he did not want to accept was the fact that he was now twenty-one years old and therefore was expected to go to work.'

But then, that would be my piece and not yours. It is very fine and sound. I only wish you felt it right to lead off as above, no mention of war experience at all.

Best season's greetings and wishes. I hope to see you some day soon, thank you for this job.

Faulkner

Why didn't he say flatly that he hadn't served in France during the war? I suspect that he was adhering to his fixed principle of never correcting misstatements about himself, though at the same time he was determined not to let these particular misstatements stand at the head of my introduction to his work. I was slow to catch the point, however, and I answered his letter by explaining briefly that some mention of his wartime experiences seemed essential if the reader was to understand his rebellion against the postwar world. Then, changing the subject, I ventured into a discussion of the Civil War in song and fiction.

I had been listening to an album of records, "Songs of the North" and "Songs of the South." The Confederate songs, I said, had disappointed me, with a few exceptions like "Eating Goober Peas," which had been sung by the starved men in the trenches at Vicksburg; most of the others seemed to have only a marginal connection with the soldiers. The Union songs, on the other hand, were immensely better than the army songs of World Wars I and II (except "Lili Marlene"), and even better than those of the volunteers in the Spanish Civil War, though the International Brigades had some good ones. The Union songs had primitively stirring melodies, ideal for a regimental band. Their lyrics, though written in clumsy doggerel, expressed the whole

75

sequence of emotion in the armies, from the first brash confidence and hurrah of "We Are Coming, Father Abram," through the boredom and grousing of the camps in northern Virginia ("They Grafted Him into the Army"), the longing for home, the grief for the dead ("There Will Be One Vacant Chair"), and the immense war weariness of the year 1864 (as revealed in "Tenting Tonight," a great song that might be sung by any army of tired veterans, fighting for any cause), to the bursting hope of "Tramp, Tramp, Tramp, the Boys Are Marching" and the wild exultation (but in a minor key) of "When Johnny Comes Marching Home." The Northern armies had sung themselves into popular legend. But eighty years later, I said—

The situation in our own time had been completely reversed. Not songs but novels about the Civil War had been pouring out in a flood, and they were mostly Southern novels. Not only were the Northern ones a minority, but most of them were feeble and conciliatory, like Hervey Allen's *Action at Aquila,* while the Southern books were defiant, dramatic, and rich in characters, so that they had easily conquered the reading public. And why this change? I asked Faulkner. Why were the Southern army songs less effective than the Northern ones (not to mention that many of them were written by Northern minstrels, like the author of "Lorena"), while the Civil War novels of our time were indubitably Southern and seemed to be winning the war that was lost at Appomattox?

In an undated letter that must have been written in the first days of January 1946, Faulkner answered my questions in his own fashion. But first he returned to the topic of what should or shouldn't be said about his part in the First World War.

Dear Cowley:

Herewith returned [the text of the introduction], with thanks. It's all right, sound and correct and penetrating. I warned you in advance I would hope for no biography, personal matter, at all. You elaborate certain theses from it, correctly I believe too. I just wish you didn't need to state in the piece the premises you derive from. If you think it necessary to include them, consider stating a simple skeleton, something like the thing in Who's Who; let the first paragraph, Section Two, read, viz:

Born (when and where). (He) came to Oxford as a child, attended Oxford grammar school without graduating, had one year as a special student in modern language in the University of Mississippi. Rest of education was undirected and uncorrelated reading. If you mention military experience at all (which is not necessary, as I could have invented a few failed RAF airmen as easily as I did Confeds) say 'belonged to RAF 1918.' Then continue: Has lived in same section of Miss. since, worked at various odd jobs until he got a job writing movies and was able to make a living at writing.

Then pick up paragraph 2 of Section II and carry on. I'm old-fashioned and probably a little mad too; I dont like having my private life and affairs available to just any and everyone who has the price of the vehicle it's printed

in, or a friend who bought it and will lend it to him.
I'll be glad to give you all the dope when we talk together.
Some of it's very funny. I just dont like it in print except
when I use it myself, like old John Sartoris and old Bayard
and Mrs Millard and Simon Strother and the other Negroes
and the dead airmen.

I don't see too much Southern legend in it [the introduc-
tion]. I'll go further than you in the harsh criticism.

The style, as you divine, is a result of the solitude, and
granted a bad one. It was further complicated by an
inherited regional or geographical (Hawthorne would say,
racial) curse. You might say, studbook style: 'by Southern
Rhetoric out of Solitude' or 'Oratory out of Solitude'.

Re. literature (songs too) in the South 1861-65. It was
probably produced but not recorded. The South was too
busy, but the main reason was probably a lack of tradition
for inventing or recording. The gentle folk hardly would.
For all their equipment for leisure (slavery, unearned
wealth) their lives were curiously completely physical,
violent, despite their physical laziness. When they were not
doing anything—not hunting or superintending farming
or riding 10 and 20 miles to visit, they really did nothing:
they slept or talked. They talked too much, I think. Oratory
was the first art; Confederate generals would hold up
attacks while they made speeches to their troops. Apart
from that, 'art' was really no manly business. It was a
polite painting of china by gentlewomen. When they
entered its domain through the doors of their libraries, it
was to read somebody else's speeches, or politics, or the
classics of the faintly school, and even these were men

who, if they had been writing men, would have written still more orations. The Negroes invented the songs and their songs were not topical nor even dated in the sense we mean.

So there was no literate middle class to produce a literature. In a pastoral cityless land they [the small farmers] lived remote and at economic war with both slave and slaveholder. When they emerged, gradually, son by infrequent son, like old Sutpen, it was not to establish themselves as a middle class but to make themselves barons too. What songs and literature they possessed back home were the old songs from 15th-16th century England and Scotland, passed from mouth to mouth because the generations couldn't write to record them. After they emerged prior to and during and after the War, they were too busy to record anything or even to sing them, probably, were ashamed of them. Pass the eighty years [1865-1945], the old unreconstructed had died off at last, the strong among the remaining realised that to survive they must stop trying to be pre 1861 barons and become a middle class, they did so, and began to create a literature.

Reason for the vital Southern one re the War and no Northern one is, the Northerner had nothing to write about regarding it. He won it. The only clean thing about War is losing it. Also, as regards material, the South was the fortunate side. That war marked a transition, the end of one age and the beginning of another, not to return. Before it in his wars man had fought man. After it, machine would fight machine. During that war, man fought barehanded against a machine. Of course that

79

doesn't explain why the North didn't use the material too. It's not enough to say that perhaps the machine which defeated his enemy was a Frankenstein which, once the Southern armies were consumed, turned on him and enslaved him and, removing him from a middle class fixed upon the land, translated him into a baronage based upon a slavery not of human beings but of machines; you cant say that because the Northerner writes about other things. Maybe the carpet-bagger is to blame, maybe it is the new blood which he brought into the South after 61 which produced the literature, and as soon as something happens to cause vast throngs of Southern middle class to move into the North, a belated Northern literature about the Civil War will spring up. Or maybe the South will be able to write all the literature about the Civil War we need and what we want is a new war, maybe a group of Dismal Swamp or Florida Everglades Abolitionists will decide to free the country from machines and will start a movement and do so, followed by a vast influx of Tennessee and Mississippi and Virginia carpet-baggers, and then the North will have a war to write about.

Thank you for seeing the piece. It's all right. The 'writing in solitude' is very true and sound. That explains a lot about my carelessness about bad taste. I am not always conscious of bad taste myself, but I am pretty sensitive to what others will call bad taste. I think I have written a lot and sent it off to print before I actually realised strangers might read it.

William Faulkner

I liked the picture of abolitionists from the Dismal Swamp invading the North to free people from machines—or was it machines from people? But I was dismayed by Faulkner's suggestion that I should omit the whole first part of the introduction; that would cost me four pages of text in which I had made what seemed to me important statements about his work. Still slow to catch the point, I wrote to explain once again why I thought it was necessary to mention his activities in wartime. Then I went back to work on some editorial notes for the book.

On January 13 I wrote to Marshall Best:

Dear Marshall:

Here are the editor's notes to precede the seven sections of the Viking Portable Faulkner. I don't know why I had such a hard time writing them; probably I had gone stale on the material—and then, on New Year's day, I came down with the damnedest case of grippe; I'm still staggering around with it, like a man with a hangover. Anyhow I think the notes do the job that is required of them. And I think that if critics will read the Faulkner, they will find an author they never met before. . . .

I'm through with the job now, except for one thing. When the page proofs are in, I'd like to spend a day in your office going through the whole business. I don't have to read it word for word, but there are some stories in which I may have neglected to iron out some little inconsistencies—

matters of words, not paragraphs, so that it would be all right to do the job on page proofs rather than galleys. . . .

As ever,

Malcolm

But there would be more to do than merely skimming through the page proofs. A few days later I received the only stern letter that Faulkner wrote me.

[Oxford] Monday. [January 21, 1946]

Dear Cowley:

Yours at hand. You're going to bugger up a fine dignified distinguished book with that war business. The only point a war reference or anecdote could serve would be to reveal me a hero, or (2) to account for the whereabouts of a male of my age on Nov. 11, 1918 in case this were a biography. If, because of some later reference back to it in the piece, you cant omit all European war reference, say only what Who's Who says and no more:

Was a member of the RAF in 1918.

I'll pay for any resetting of type, plates, alteration, etc.

I dont think I can come up East this spring. I'll have to go back to Warner by 15 Mar. or have his legal dogs on me. He has already made vague though dire threats about warning any editor to buy my stuff at his peril, if I dont come back.

[I had told him that a literary friend, Thomas Mabry, was leaving the East and was moving back to Tennessee, where he had bought a large farm. Faulkner continued:] If Thomas is taking up farming cold at his age, even with 372 acres, I hope he's rich; he'll need to be. He'd better move his decimal point and start with 3.72 acres. If he really wants a farm, I'll sell him mine, including 4 span of mules and 11 head of niggers.

I'm really concerned about the war reference. As I said last, I'm going to be proud of this book. I wouldn't have put in anything at all about the war or any other personal matter.

Yours,
Faulkner

This time I saw the light. In a letter to the Viking Press, I asked them to delete the statement that Faulkner's plane had been damaged in combat. It was too late to make extensive changes, but Faulkner was relieved by the correction of this one gross error. He wrote:

[Oxford] Friday. [February 1, 1946]

Dear Cowley:

Yours of 26th at hand. I see your point now about the war business, and granting the value of the parallel you will infer, it is 'structurally' necessary. I dont like the paragraph because it makes me out more of a hero than

I was, and I am going to be proud of your book. The mishap was caused not by combat but by (euphoniously) 'cockpit trouble'; i.e., my own foolishness; the injury I suffered I still feel I got at bargain rates. A lot of that sort of thing happened in those days, the culprit unravelling himself from the subsequent unauthorised crash incapable of any explanation as far as advancing the war went, and grasping at any frantic straw before someone in authority would want to know what became of the aeroplane, would hurry to the office and enter it in the squadron records as 'practice flight'. As compared with men I knew, friends I had and lost, I deserve no more than the sentence I suggested before: 'served in (or belonged to) RAF'. But I see where your paragraph will be better for your purpose, and I am sorry it's not nearer right.

I just had a letter from Linscott [then the senior editor at Random House] about the proposed re-issue. I may write him, suggest your idea of [*The Sound and the Fury*] alone, plus the Compson thing you have. He wants an introduction for it, for $250.00. I'll do almost anything for $250.00 or even $25.00, but I dont know how to write introductions. I dont recall ever seeing one, except the one I wrote for B Cerf about 10 years ago when he thought he would reprint TSAF and didn't or forgot it or whatever.

I would like to come up East, but I am about to run out of money and will have to go back to Cal. I am afraid. But if I can come up, I'll certainly let you know.

How much land will you work? If you are now a tractor man, it must be more than just a shirt-tail of it.

                                                    Faulkner

I had told him about buying a little tractor. Now I had to explain that it was a *very* little tractor, the size of a one-horse plow, and that I would use it to cultivate a garden smaller than a tennis court. More important, I sent him a revised first paragraph of my introduction, with the account of his military service reduced to ten accurate words: "He had served in the Royal Air Force in 1918."

Before my letter reached him, Faulkner had written me about another subject.

[Oxford] Tuesday. [February 5, 1946]

Dear Cowley:

I have a letter from Linscott about the combined TSAF and LAY DYING. I wrote him to include the new material in the appendix which you have. I dont have a clear copy of it. Could you have a copy made, I will pay the score, and send it to Linscott? Damn to hell, I have never yet been able to afford a secretary; I never missed one much until these last few years. Now I dont know where about half of what I have is, nor even (at times) whether I ever wrote it or not.

Let me hear if possible to get a copy of the appendix.

A few days later I wrote a long letter to Linscott that casts a sidelight on the Faulkner story.

February 12, 1946

Dear Bob:

Letter from Faulkner. I gather from it (1) that you have decided to go ahead with the combination Modern Library volume containing two of his novels, "The Sound and the Fury" and "As I Lay Dying"; (2) that you asked him to write an introduction to it (I don't know what he answered); that you want to include (3) the appendix he wrote for the Viking Portable (of which he hasn't a copy; he asked for mine).

Today I'm sending him the text of his appendix. On this text, Viking holds the copyright, and you'll have to write Marshall Best for permission to use it; but on such matters Viking is very obliging, and I don't anticipate any difficulty there. Another, auctorial, difficulty does exist, however, and I'm writing Faulkner about it. He hasn't any copy of "The Sound and the Fury," having sent his one personal copy to Random House some years ago, he says—and therefore he wrote the appendix from his memory of the novel. His memory was faulty at two or three points, so that the appendix has some inconsistencies with the novel that any reader would remark if they were printed in the same volume (they won't remark it in the Viking Portable, however, since I used only 12,000 words of the novel). I'm going to lend him my copy of TSATF and tell him that he has to do some rewriting. But that's only a temporary loan. You guys at Random House will have to get him a copy of the book somehow—either dig up the one he sent to Random House several years ago, or else advertise in Publishers' Weekly (and be lucky to get an answer, because TSATF isn't findable even in the second-hand bookstores), or else hijack a copy from some friend.

I hope he said he wouldn't write an introduction. He's no good at writing introductions, to judge from the little piece he did for the Modern Library edition of "Sanctuary." That piece hurt him with the critics, because they hate to find that they had praised a book which the author himself says was only written for money. (Zamatterafack, Faulkner first wrote it for money, then rewrote it carefully, something one only discovered from reading his introduction more attentively.) A lot of people (not me) would be glad to write a short introduction to the book you are planning to publish. I mention among other names: Conrad Aiken (maybe the best for the job, if he's not on bad terms with Random . . .); Kay Boyle (a Faulkner enthusiast); Ernest Hemingway (though an introduction by him might be in dubious taste—but he has a lot to say about Faulkner, mostly on the credit side); and my own choice for the job, to whom you would probably say No—Jean-Paul Sartre, whose reputation here is going to spread, who acknowledges Faulkner as his master, and who is the best critic, except Malraux, perhaps, now writing in any language (he is in New York again, I hear).

I'm still dubious about the book you are planning as the best way to start Faulkner back into general circulation. The dubiety comes from questions in my own mind about "As I Lay Dying," which, disagreeing with Faulkner, I haven't ever regarded as one of his best novels. Too much shifting about from one stream of consciousness to another. Not enough contrast with TSATF, both being stream-of-consciousness novels. I'd much prefer, let us say, "The Wild Palms," to give a better picture of Faulkner's range. "The Wild Palms" is a short novel too, under 80,000 words. Also, I think it's a great pity that you are planning to issue the book next fall. Viking is putting a good deal of money into the Faulkner Portable—doing a very careful job on it—letting it run to 750 pages, as against the 600 they usually allot to a living author—printing a new map of Yoknapatawpha County as an end paper—and if the book gets reviews (as I hope it will) and shows any sign of selling, and *if* Viking is sure of an unobstructed year of sales, they might make a good advertising appropriation too, as they did for the Hemingway —and *then* the way would really be prepared for a reissue of Faulkner's other books. This business of re-launching him requires cooperation rather than rivalry.

I'm anxious for you to see the job I did on the book. It looks good to me now, and I hope the critics will agree with me.

As ever,
Malcolm

My letter to Linscott proved to be grandly ineffective. Random House went ahead with its plan to reprint *The Sound and the Fury* and *As I Lay Dying* in the same Modern Library volume. It appeared in the fall of 1946—as it should have done; my objection on this point was well meant, but not well taken. The volume has no introduction by Sartre or anyone else. It does include Faulkner's Appendix, in a slightly different version from the one that appears in the *Portable*. Faulkner had worked a little more on it; he had accepted some of my emendations, rejected others, and revised his entry on Jason Compson. He had not attempted, however, to resolve the several discrepancies between the Appendix and the earlier text of the novel.

This refusal to be consistent was for a reason that I have already suggested, but Faulkner would state it explicitly at the end of his next letter.

[Oxford] Monday. [February 18, 1946]

Dear Brother:

I feel much better about the book with your foreword beginning as now. I saw your point about (and need for) the other opening all the time. But to me it was false. Not factually, I dont care much for facts, am not much interested in them, you cant stand a fact up, you've got to prop it up, and when you move to one side a little and look at it from that angle, it's not thick enough to cast a shadow in that direction. But in truth, though maybe what I mean by truth is humility and maybe what I think is humility is really immitigable pride, I would have preferred nothing at all prior to the instant I began to write, as though Faulkner and Typewriter were concomitant, coadjutant and without past on the moment they first faced each other at the suitable (nameless) table.

I cant write an introduction; I hope to hell Random House cant find the other one I did. What about doing

it yourself? or would that be too much Cowley plus
F.? Let me know about it. I will then write Linscott
and ask for someone to do it. I dont want to read TSAF
again [by then I had sent him my treasured copy of
the novel]. Would rather let the appendix stand with
the inconsistencies, perhaps make a statement (quotable)
at the end of the introduction, viz.: The inconsistencies in
the appendix prove that to me the book is still alive after
15 years, and being still alive is growing, changing;
the appendix was done at the same heat as the book,
even though 15 years later, and so it is the book itself
which is inconsistent: not the appendix. That is, at the
age of 30 I did not know these people as at 45 I now do;
that I was even wrong now and then in the very con-
clusions I drew from watching them, and the information in which I once believed. (I believe I was 28 when I
wrote the book. That's almost 20 years.)

I will return your volume carefully.

Faulkner

I didn't hear from him again for two months. Meanwhile
the book was being printed, and bound copies were ready
by the middle of April. The author wrote me a few days
later.

[Oxford] Tuesday. [April 23, 1946]

Dear Cowley:
    The job is splendid. Damn you to hell anyway. But
even if I had beat you to the idea, mine wouldn't have

been this good. By God, I didn't know myself what I had tried to do, and how much I had succeeded.

I am asking Viking to send me more copies (I had just one) and I want to sign one for you, if you are inclined. Spotted horses is pretty funny, after a few years.

Random House and [Harold] Ober lit a fire under Warner, I dont know how, and I am here until September anyway, on a dole from Random House, working at what seems now to me to be my magnum o.

Faulkner

It was the handsomest letter of acknowledgment I had ever received. But the treasure I have saved from those days is the copy of *The Sound and the Fury* that I sent him because he had no copy of his own. It came back with an inscription:

To Malcolm Cowley——
Who beat me to what was to have been the leisurely pleasure
of my old age.

William Faulkner

VI

The question was whether the book would be reviewed. At first I was afraid that it would be noticed briefly or passed over in silence like some of the earlier Portables, but I should have felt more confidence in Faulkner's standing among his fellow novelists. Many of these, as I knew already, were disturbed by what then appeared to be a critical conspiracy against him. A few would be almost certain to seize upon the Portable as an occasion for putting their admiration on record.

Caroline Gordon was the first. She was familiar with the background of Faulkner's novels, she could speak with authority about his technical achievements, and, as another Southern novelist whose best work had been neglected, she could plead his cause with more than a little personal feeling. Her review appeared surprisingly on the front page of the *New York Times Book Review,* and it made me feel that the Faulkner revival was under way. The other early reviews of the book, though favorable, were mostly short and weightless. In August, however, a second novelist came forward, this time in the *New Republic,* where he wrote at such length that his review, or essay, had to be continued in the following issue of the magazine.

The second novelist was Robert Penn Warren, and I found that his appraisal of Faulkner's work was the fairest that anyone had offered. What he said about the Negro characters in the Yoknapatawpha novels seemed to me especially discerning. Warren praised my introduction, but with a few reservations that I was, incidentally, quite willing to accept. The chief reservation concerned my statement of Faulkner's theme, which I had interpreted as a legend of the South. Warren said that the interpretation "should be somewhat modified, at least in emphasis." It was important, he continued, "that Faulkner's work be regarded, not in terms of the South against the North, but in terms of issues which are common to our modern world. The legend is not merely a legend of the South, but is also a legend of our general plight and problem." That is almost what Faulkner himself had told me in an early letter, the one he wrote in November 1944, and my introduction should have made it clearer that he was using his Southern material to suggest a broadly human situation.

The end of Warren's review was a summons to critics and scholars.

The study of Faulkner [he said] is the most challenging single task in contemporary American literature for criticism to undertake. Here is a novelist who, in mass of work, in scope of material, in range of effect, in reportorial accuracy and symbolic subtlety, in philosophical weight, can be put beside the masters of our own past literature. Yet this accomplishment has been effected in what almost amounts to critical isolation and silence, and when the silence has been broken it has usually been broken by someone (sometimes one of our better critics) whose reading has been hasty, whose analysis unscholarly and whose judgments superficial. The picture of Faulkner presented to the public by such criticism is a combination of Thomas Nelson Page, a fascist, and a psychopath gnawing his nails. Of course, this picture is usually accompanied by a grudging remark about genius.

Cowley's book, for its intelligence, sensitivity, and sobriety in the introduction, and for the ingenuity and judgment exhibited in the selections, would be valuable at any time. But it is especially valuable at this time. Perhaps it can mark a turning point in Faulkner's reputation. That will be of slight service to Faulkner, who, as much as any writer of our place and time, can rest in confidence. He can afford to wait. But can we?

By issuing that challenge to academic critics, Warren introduced a new element into the situation. American literary scholarship has always been affected by changing fashions in subject matter. In those days all the brilliant graduate students were explicating T. S. Eliot, so it seemed, unless they were writing dissertations on the minor works of Herman Melville; they would scarcely admit that anyone else was worthy of being closely read. Warren's advice, however, carried weight in the academic world. Very soon one began to hear of Faulkner studies, most of them initiated by venturesome scholars in universities scattered through the South and the Midwest. Later, as the production of studies continued year by year, one would come to think of a river fed and swollen by tributaries from lonely glens until it swept across the plain in a sustained flood.

Already in the spring of 1946 I was learning more about Faulkner's European reputation, which, as I have suggested, was the result of an earlier and independent growth. Ilya Ehrenburg, with two other Soviet writers, had been invited to this country by the State Department; they arrived at the end of April. After receiving a rather mysterious invitation by telephone, I paid a visit to Ehrenburg's small room at the Waldorf. He was a big man with a pale skin, intensely black eyes, and a confusion of black hair touched with gray. As I listened to his idiomatic French and watched him stab out one cigarette after another, he seemed to me less Russian than Central European, less the man of letters than the international journalist: sharp-witted, universally informed, and sensitive to the latest currents of opinion. It turned out that I was there to be asked questions about Faulkner. Was he really as great a writer as Ehrenburg judged him to be after reading two or three of his novels in French? How did he stand on the Negro question? What would be the best way of introducing his work to the Russian public? *"C'est un problème bougrement difficile,"* Ehrenburg said, alluding vaguely to the problems created for Russian publishers by the hard-line Communists. Then another question: How could he meet Faulkner? He had sent him a letter, but had received no answer. At present he planned simply to visit Oxford and take his chances.

I promised to write Faulkner and announce the visit. But he didn't like to meet strangers, I told Ehrenburg, and I couldn't promise what his answer would be. Then we fell to discussing the international situation, about which Ehrenburg was somber. He could already hear the first rumblings of the Cold War.

I wrote as promised. Faulkner's answer, which arrived a few days later, was a mixture of dismay with two parts of indignation.

95

[Oxford] [May 1946]

Dear friend:

Thank you for warning me. What the hell can I do? Goddam it I've spent almost fifty years trying to cure myself of the curse of human speech, all for nothing. Last month two damned swedes, two days ago a confounded Chicago reporter, and now this one that cant even speak english. As if anything he or I either know, or both of us together know, is worth being said once, let alone twice through an interpreter. I swear to christ being in hollywood was better than this where nobody knew me or cared a damn. I hate like hell to be in this state, I can even put up with mankind when I have time to adjust. But I do like to have the chance to invite people to come to look at me and see where I keep my tail or my other head or whatever it is strangers want to come here for.

Thank you again for warning; I'll just have to bull through it someway. The book received. [It was a copy of the Portable that I had inscribed to Faulkner, and he was inscribing another copy to me.] Yours in mail tomorrow. Maybe the b hasn't realised he's in America now; I still own my home.

Faulkner

Ehrenburg spent two weeks traveling through the South in a Buick convertible, with two American friends and a young man from the State Department. He visited Oxford, and Faulkner didn't see him. The incident had no repercussions. As for the "two damned swedes" mentioned in the letter, they were another token of the disproportion between Faulkner's American and his European reputation. Later I learned that they were correspondents on the track of an exclusive story. They came to Oxford because friends in Stockholm had passed on to them the sensational rumor that Faulkner was being considered for the Nobel Prize. Americans would scarcely have believed the rumor in 1946, at a time when his books—except for the Portable and, I think, a new printing of *Sanctuary*—were still out of print in this country.

In December I sent him an appeal for funds to be distributed in China through the Chinese Writers' Association. It was before the Communists took over the country, but civil war was already raging in Manchuria, and wartime censorship had been reimposed by the Nationalist government. More than two hundred magazines and newspapers had been closed down, mostly in Shanghai and Peiping, with the result that many established writers were living on the edge of starvation. The appeal for funds to help them was signed by the president of the P.E.N. Club and half a dozen members with a special interest in Chinese affairs. Faulkner answered it with a personal letter.

[Oxford] Sunday. [December, 1946]
Dear Brother:

Thank you for sending me the Chinese thing. Will see about it. I am still here in Miss. since Sept 1945 now. Am on Random House's cuff, to write a book, wont go back to Cal. until Random House gets tired and money ceases. I shall get back to work at it, now that the weather's too bad here to hunt. I missed a beautiful stag last fall. He had what you call 6 points and we here 12, since we count both horns of the antlers. He broke out of a thicket at full speed; I just heard a stick crack and looked around and there he was, running flat like a horse, not jumping at all, about 30 mph, about 100 yards away. He ran in full sight for 50 yards. I think perhaps the first bullet (it was a .270) hit a twig and blew up. But the second shot I missed him clean. He was running too fast for me. He was a beautiful sight. Now it's done, I'm glad his head is still in the woods instead of on a plank on the wall.

It's a dull life here. . . . But if I leave here I will spend in two weeks money I can live here for two months on, and then I'd have to go back to Cal. At 30 you become aware suddenly that you have become the slave of [a] vast and growing mass of inanimate junk, possessions; you dont dare look at any of it too closely because you'll have to admit there is not one piece of it you really want. But you bear it for the next eighteen years because you still believe you will escape from it someday. Then one day you are almost 50 and you know you never will.

Faulkner

The correspondence lapsed for more than a year, and it was not until the summer of 1948 that I received an unexpected query.

Oxford, Miss.
16 July

Dear Brother Cowley:

I had a letter from a Mr Pearson at New Haven about
coming there to make a talk, something. I have lost it
and cant answer. He spoke of you in the letter; will you
either send me his address or if you correspond write
him my apologies for losing the address and that I dont
think I know anything worth 200 dollars worth talking
about but I hope to be up East this fall though I still
dont believe I will know anything to talk about worth
200 dollars so I would probably settle for a bottle of good
whiskey.

If I come up, I would like to see you.

Faulkner

RFD Gaylordsville, Conn.[1]
July 20, 1948.

Dear Brother Faulkner:

The man at Yale is Professor Norman Holmes Pearson
and his address is simply c/o Yale Graduate School,
New Haven. He's out in California now, but a letter
would be forwarded. . . . He helped me a lot with the
Portable Hawthorne I was working on last winter. It's
out now—or will be out this week—and I want to send
you a copy as soon as I get one, hoping that you'll
read it, for there are some curious points of similarity

---

[1] I was living in Sherman, as always, but our little town had no post office
until 1949 or thereabouts. Mail came from Gaylordsville by rural carrier.

between your work and Hawthorne's, in spite of the differences.

I'm working just now on a profile of Hemingway. Last spring I went down to see him with the family—wife & son—expenses paid by *Life*.

When you get North you'll find that you're not a neglected author any longer, that they're studying you in the colleges, including Yale, where lots of the kids think that "The Bear" is the greatest story ever written, and that you'll have to resign yourself to bearing the expense of greatness, which is a pretty high expense. Hemingway loves being a great man, it's something he needs and demands, and nobody begrudges it to him because he keeps paying for it at every moment in terms of kindness and attention and thoughtfulness to anyone around him. He lives like old Father Abraham in the midst of his flocks and herds and servants and wives and children and friends and dependents, watching out for them, teaching and advising them, writing them letters—and meanwhile screwing the big motion-picture people so that he can get money to maintain his retinue. He just sold an almost unfilmable short story, "The Snows of Kilimanjaro," to the movies for $125,000. It's a curious life for a writer (though Mark Twain lived something like that) and Hemingway is a curious and very likable person and drinks enough to put almost anyone else in the alcoholic ward—then spends much of the night reading because he can't sleep and goes to work in the morning on the big novel he's had around for seven or eight years and doesn't know when he'll

finish; I think he's got buck fever about that novel;
it *has* to be good when it comes out, and either he'll keep
working on it until it *is* good or else he'll somehow
manage never to finish it. You would stifle and go crazy
in the mob that surrounds him—and yet when you
come North you're going to have your experience of being
admired and flattered; and you might as well get ready
to face it, because it's one of the things you bargained
for, part of the stuff in fine print that was on the contract
you signed when you became a writer, a hell of a long
time since.

I went to a local party last week end and a drunk
whom I like walled me off in a corner to talk about
Faulkner. First he praised the Portable and then he became belligerent. "Why, you bastard," he said, "why
did you say that 'Spotted Horses' was as good as Mark
Twain? Couldn't you see that it was twice as funny
as anything Mark Twain ever wrote?" Well, I ducked
out of that one by mixing him another drink; but you
can see how things are going. My uncalled-for advice:
just keep away from big parties, from fools and old
women, and everything will be swell.

I talk as if your trip was all settled and I see by your note
that it isn't. I'd like you to find time for a day or two
here [in Sherman] if you can make it—it's nice in the
fall in these parts, especially after the summer soldiers
have gone back to NY. . . . Do let me know in advance when you're coming, because I might be spending
the month of October at Yaddo and I'd like to come
down when you arrive.

Two questions meanwhile: what's the novel that's coming out this fall (I'll have to review it), and is the other novel, the one about World War I, finished yet? And a mild speculation: why shouldn't the movies buy some of your old stories, the way they buy Hemingway's, so that you wouldn't have to work for the bastards any more?

As ever,
Cowley

Faulkner didn't answer the letter. In October his new book was published, the first since *Go Down, Moses* in 1942 (though meanwhile not a few of the earlier books had been reissued). The new one was *Intruder in the Dust,* and I reviewed it for the *New Republic.* I said that the story—or rather the sermon that one of the characters, Gavin Stevens, interpolated into the story—revealed the dilemma of Southern nationalism. "The tragedy of intelligent Southerners like Stevens (or like Faulkner)," I concluded, "is that their two fundamental beliefs, in equal justice and in Southern independence (or simple identity) are now in violent conflict."

Toward the end of the month Faulkner made his promised visit to New York. My wife and I were invited to a dinner given to celebrate his arrival. That would be our first meeting.

VII

When I was working on the profile of Hemingway in the summer of 1948, my editor at *Life,* Robert Coughlan, had asked me whether I would undertake a companion piece on Faulkner. "That depends," I said, "on whether Faulkner consents to have it written. I'll ask him when he comes to New York, and in the meantime I'll start collecting material."

Accordingly I made some very long entries in my notebook during Faulkner's October visit. Here I shall set them down without correcting some errors and repetitions.

Sunday, October 23.—This week William Faulkner has been in NY. There was a dinner for him Tuesday evening at the Park Avenue apartment of Robert Haas [a partner in Random House]—a dinner with two butlers hired for the occasion, one of those dinners in style (though nobody dressed) where the ladies withdraw as they did fifty years ago and leave the gentlemen discoursing over cigars and cognac. There was a good deal of cognac. Muriel [my wife] and I left at two in the morning, but it seems that Faulkner and Eric Devine and perhaps one or two others adjourned to Hal Smith's apartment.

Faulkner is a small man (5 ft. 5, I should judge), very

neatly put together, slim and muscular. Small, beautifully shaped hands. His face has an expression like Poe's in photographs, crooked and melancholy. But his forehead is low, his nose Roman, and his gray hair forms a low wreath around his forehead, so that he also looks like a Roman emperor. Bushy eyebrows; eyes deeply set and with a droop at the outer corners; a bristly mustache. He stands or walks with an air of great dignity and talks—tells stories—in a strong Mississippi accent.

Apparently his farm 17 (?) miles out of Oxford is a large one, with part of it under cultivation by three Negro families whom he trusts. Each family has ten acres for its own use, planted in cotton right up to the doorstep; he buys the cotton. His own business is raising beef cattle and feed for the cattle (outside of the acres in cultivation, the rest of the farm is grazed). The Negro families keep their own accounts of how much they work for him.

He thinks Hemingway has no courage *to experiment*. "You have to take chances and put it down good or bad," he says of his own writing. "Some time," he also says, "you have to go off by yourself and write. Last spring I finished *Intruder in the Dust* in three months."

I remember setting down those notes on a gray and shivery Sunday morning. That afternoon I drove to New York, saw Faulkner again, and brought him back with me to Sherman. The next entry in the notebook was made on Tuesday.

October 25.—Faulkner is 51 years old, weighs 148 pounds,

and his waist is so slim that he can wear Robbie's old pants.
[Robbie, then in his first year at boarding school, was thirteen and had outgrown the pants.] A small head, very dark
brown eyes. One eyebrow goes up, the other down, and
perhaps that is what gives him the resemblance to Poe. Hair
lies close to his head and is ringleted like a Roman gentle-
man's.

We talked about my notion that he should arrange his
stories by subject matter and have them printed in one big
volume, preferably with a foreword. He promised to think
about it. Then he told me about his new novel, of which he
has written 500 pages. It is about Christ in the French army,
a corporal with a squad of 12 men—and a general who is
Antichrist and takes him up on a hill and offers him the
world. Symbolic and unreal, except for 300 wild pages about
a three-legged racehorse in Tennessee. Mary Magdalene and
the other two Marys. There is a strange mutiny in which the
soldiers on both sides simply refuse to fight. The corporal's
body is chosen for that of the Unknown Soldier. Christ (or
his disciple) lives again in the crowd.

He has an idea for the jacket of the novel. Instead of carry-
ing the usual title, illustration, and descriptive text, it would
show nothing but a cross—with perhaps below it in the
right-hand corner, and not in large type, the two words "A
Fable." [Apparently, if Faulkner's idea had been carried out,
the novel would not have been *A Fable*. Its real title, shown
as in a rebus, would have been *The Cross: A Fable*. But his
publishers must have objected that librarians have found no
way of listing rebuses alphabetically in their card catalogues.]

We talked about Hollywood. In 1942 when he owed a big

bill at the grocer's, he wrote to Warner Brothers and said he'd work for whatever they gave him, if they paid his way to Hollywood. They paid his way, and he signed a contract that started at $100 a week and covered seven years (with raises, but not big ones; he's now getting $500 a week when he works for Warner).

He got screen credit for *The Big Sleep* and *To Have and Have Not*. He thinks his best picture was *The Southerner,* done with Jean Renoir [for which Faulkner didn't get credit]. He says that he doesn't really know the trade, but always has a highly skilled collaborator who suggests "the business"—like Bogart's tossing a book of matches to Bacall when he meets her (in *To Have and Have Not*) to show that he regards her as a tramp; Faulkner wouldn't have thought of that. The collaborator got $2500 a week, incidentally. Mostly Faulkner has done jobs for Howard Hawks, and likes him. He has been a sort of play doctor for Hawks, working with him on the set, inventing new scenes and writing new dialogue.

He told me about the old Negro woman who had nursed him and who died some years ago after she had a stroke from eating green watermelon.[1] Her children and grand-

---

[1] *Go Down, Moses* (1942) bears the following dedication:

To Mammy
CAROLINE BARR
Mississippi
[1840-1940]
Who was born in slavery and who/gave to my family a fidelity without/stint or calculation of recompense/and to my childhood an immeasur-/able devotion and love

She was buried from the Faulkner parlor, and Faulkner himself gave the funeral address.

children and great-grandchildren gathered round her bed; then she rallied and lived for a time as a family tyrant. Late at night Faulkner would hear soft shuffling feet on the outside stairs and a strange Negro voice would say, "She wants ice cream." So he would dress and drive perhaps 40 miles to find an open drugstore where he could buy ice cream. He tries to do what he can for Negroes—not for "the Negro." He caused a mild scandal at Ole Miss when he said that Negroes should attend the university.

Very modest. Takes suggestions if they are offered in good part. Has a Southerner's extremely good manners. Also has an extreme sense of privacy. Doesn't want his private life in the public prints.

We had been talking about the profile of him that *Life* had asked me to do. I thought it should deal chiefly with his work, and that the biographical details might be limited to those already published in magazines or newspapers. Faulkner wasn't happy about the intrusion into his life, modest and circumspect as it promised to be, but when we went back to the subject, after lunch on Tuesday, he gave what I interpreted as a sigh of resigned assent. It was a magnificent fall afternoon. The maples had lost most of their leaves, but the oaks still wore an imperial purple. We went for a long drive across the foothills of the Taconic Range into the Harlem Valley, which is like a continuation northward of the Shenandoah. Between comments on the landscape, Faulkner brought forth a good deal of information about himself, as if to help along my project. He continued to talk about himself that evening, and some of the information went into the next entry in my notebook.

October 26, Faulkner Again.—He's gone now, by train for New York. . . . I want to set down a few of the things he told us (1) about his life in Oxford and New Orleans after the war, and his first book; (2) about the South; (3) about writing.

1. After the war he traveled around the country with a friend and drinking companion who was the receiver for a big bankrupt lumber company. Sometimes he was called an assistant, sometimes a secretary, and he was about to go to Cuba as an interpreter (he didn't know Spanish) when Stark Young told him that he ought to try living in NY and promised to get him a job at Lord & Taylor's bookstore. He worked there several months for $11 a week and lived in a room for which he paid $2.50 a week. Then he got a letter from home telling him that he had been appointed postmaster.

After working as postmaster for about two years, he went to New Orleans and became a rum runner. He ran a cabin cruiser out to where he got the alcohol, took it into the city through bayous, and delivered it to the back room of an Italian restaurant. There the proprietor's mother, a woman of 80, took charge of it and gave it the proper flavors: laudanum, if it was to be called Scotch, and creosote, if it was to be rye. She couldn't read, but she knew the labels by the looks of them.

In New Orleans he met his old boss at Lord & Taylor's,

Elizabeth Prall, and found that she was now Mrs. Sherwood Anderson. He used to go walking with Anderson in the afternoon and drink with him all night. He thought, "If this is the way a writer lives, I want to be a writer." He told Mrs. Anderson that he was writing a book. She said, "Don't you ask Sherwood to read it." Then she said, "But I'll read it," and he finally gave her the ms. Before that time Sherwood had said, expecting his publisher in New Orleans, "If you promise that I won't have to read it, I'll make Horace Liveright publish it."

Bill went for a walking trip in France and Italy. When he was back in Paris, broke, he got a letter from Liveright with a check for $200, his advance. Nobody would cash the check for him. The American consul told him to send it back to Liveright and ask for a draft. But he went to the British consul, showed him his British army dogtag, and the consul gave him the $200. When he got back to Oxford the book, *Soldier's Pay,* had been published and forgotten.

He says that he commenced with the idea that novels should deal with imaginary scenes and people—so *Soldier's Pay* was laid in Georgia, where he had never been. With *Sartoris,* his third novel, he began to create Yoknapatawpha County. He started with the characters; then they required a background, which he imagined, and the background suggested other characters. When he was writing *The Sound and the Fury,* he found there were connections between the Sartoris family and the Compsons, and from that point the county continued to grow. Several times its location has shifted a few miles westward. It borrows scenes and features from three real Mississippi counties.

2. *The South.*—"Mississippi is still the frontier," he says. "In Mississippi an officer of the law can't go around without a gun where he can reach it fast because he never knows when he's going to need it." The Southern or frontier way, he says, is to have not enough, but always more than enough, enough to waste. Cut down a tree to make a linchpin.

Speaking of the Southern sense of family, "That's also a memory of the frontier. It goes back to the days when kin were all you had to depend on for help, because you couldn't depend on the law. But it's also a memory of the Highland clans."

His section of Mississippi is Scotch, Highland and Lowland, inhabited by the descendants of men who crossed the mountains from North Carolina, on horseback or on foot. Faulkner's great-grandfather Murry, who lived to be a hundred, spoke Gaelic. When his old wife berated him, he used to go up to his room, dress in his kilt, buckle on his claymore, and come down and sulk in the chimney corner. The Falkners, to use the earlier spelling of the name, were Lowlanders. Colonel William Falkner, Bill's great-grandfather, wrote *The White Rose of Memphis,* which was sold by train butchers all over the South. It was somewhat ungrammatical, says the author's great-grandson; Colonel Falkner believed that all pronouns should be in the nominative case.

We talked about *Intruder in the Dust,* though without mentioning my review; I assumed that he hadn't read it. Still, what he said about Gavin Stevens may have been an indirect answer to my interpretation of the novel. Stevens, he explained, was not speaking for the author, but for the best type of liberal Southerners; that is how they feel about the

Negroes. "If the race problems were just left to the children," Faulkner told me, "they'd be solved soon enough. It's the grown-ups and especially the women who keep the prejudice alive."

His farm is run by the three Negro tenant families, in which there are five hands. He lets them have the profits, if any, because—he said, speaking very softly— "The Negroes don't always get a square deal in Mississippi." He figures that his beef costs him $5 a pound.

Counties in Mississippi are divided into "beats," which correspond to townships in the Midwest. Each beat has a supervisor, who determines which roads are to be improved. Roads with a lot of voters on them get more attention. Behind Faulkner's farm is an old plantation broken up into little freeholdings owned by Negroes. There isn't a vote in the two or three miles between the highway and the river, and therefore there isn't a road—although the Negro tenants and freeholders work to keep a fair-weather trace open through his land.

He belongs to a hunting club composed mostly of old men who spend the last week of November hunting deer on horseback, with dogs, in a patch of wilderness down in the Delta. I asked whether they hunted bear, thinking of his marvelous story, and he said, "No, the last bear disappeared from the Delta after the big flood in 1927."— If he makes a trip to NY it will be in the middle fall; then he goes back to get his crop in; then hunting in the Delta; then the family reunion at Christmastime.

3. *On writing.* "Get it down. Take chances. It may be bad, but that's the only way you can do anything really good.

"Wolfe took the most chances, although he didn't always know what he was doing. I come next and then Dos Passos. Hemingway doesn't take chances enough."

Faulkner works when he feels like working, sometimes for 12 or 13 hours a day. Usually he works in the morning, but when the mood is on him he works in the afternoons too, and at night. I think he writes in pencil, then copies and corrects on a very old typewriter (see his story of how he wrote *As I Lay Dying* on the bottom of a wheelbarrow). "Some time you've got to go to work and finish it," he said.

That was in the evening after our return from the Harlem Valley. He got out of his chair and began pacing up and down the living room. With his short steps and small features, he gave an impression of delicacy, fastidiousness, but also of humility combined with something close to Napoleonic pride. "My ambition," he said, "is to put everything into one sentence—not only the present but the whole past on which it depends and which keeps overtaking the present, second by second." He went on to explain that in writing his prodigious sentences he is trying to convey a sense of simultaneity, not only giving what happened in the shifting moment but suggesting everything that went before and made the quality of that moment.

I asked him about *Go Down, Moses,* a book that was published with a subtitle, "and Other Stories." [2] It had always impressed me, I said, as being essentially a novel. When it appeared in 1942, there was a general notion in the publish-

---

[2] The subtitle disappeared, at Faulkner's request, when *Go Down, Moses* was reprinted in 1949.

ing world that a collection of stories would have about one-third the sale of a novel by the same author, and the result was that many such collections were thinly disguised as novels. *Go Down, Moses,* I ventured, was the only instance on record of a novel that masqueraded as a collection of stories.

"I always *thought* it was a novel," Faulkner said.

There were seven stories in the book, I continued, and six of them dealt with the descendants, black and white, of old Carothers McCaslin. The only one that fell outside the novelistic pattern was "Pantaloon in Black," the story of an immensely powerful Negro who went mad with grief when his wife died.

"Oh, you mean the story about Rider?" Faulkner said. "Rider was one of the McCaslin Negroes."

It was no use asking, "Why didn't you say so?"

He told me that his mother wanted him to be a painter. Sometimes he does paint a little, not with a brush—"I have no patience for that"—but with a kitchen knife. If he had the money he would hire a fresco painter to do some of the scenes in his books—for example, the Chickasaws dragging the steamboat through the woods on rollers, while The Man sits on deck in the red shoes too small for his feet (as in "A Justice"), or the scene from *Absalom, Absalom!* in which the French architect, hiding in a swamp, is discovered and held cowering in a circle of torches by Sutpen and his half-naked slaves.

Today I drove him to Brewster for the late-morning train. Although the rest of his clothes are expensive and well cared for, he wears a very old and shabby English army-officer's trench coat. I suspect that it is the same one he wore in 1918, in the RAF, and later in New Orleans when he carried a volume of Shakespeare in one of the big slash pockets and a bottle of whisky in the other. This morning he carried only a book, which he asked to borrow and I invited him to keep, a paperback copy of *The Lost Weekend*.

I remember two of the remarks about writing that he made on the long drive. In regard to style he said, "There are some kinds of writing that you have to do very fast, like riding a bicycle on a tightrope." Later I mentioned Hawthorne's complaint about the devil who got into his inkpot. "I listen to the voices," Faulkner told me, "and when I put down what the voices say, it's right. Sometimes I don't like what they say, but I don't change it."

On Friday I went to New York, where I had lunch with Faulkner and his editor Saxe Commins. On Saturday afternoon, when I was back in Sherman, the florist from New Milford, eight miles away, arrived with a dozen long-stemmed roses that Faulkner had ordered for my wife. By that time he was on his way to Oxford, as I learned from his next letter.

Oxford, Monday. [November 1, 1948]

Dear Malcolm:

I had a slow uneventful trip down on a flight which stopped everywhere there was an airport big enough, but I was home in my own bed by midnight Saturday.

It wasn't too dull because I spent the time thinking about the collection of stories, the which the more I think about, the better I like. The only book foreword I ever remembered was one I read when I was about sixteen I suppose, in one of Sienckewicz (maybe that's not even spelled right), which, I dont even remember: Pan Michael or what, nor the actual words either: something like 'This book written in . . . [Faulkner's punctuation] travail (he may have said even agony and sacrifice) for the uplifting of men's hearts.'[3] Which I believe is the one worthwhile purpose of any book and so even to a collection of short stories, form, integration, is as important

---

[3] Henryk Sienkiewicz (1846-1916) was the first Polish writer to be awarded the Nobel Prize. In this country he is remembered, if at all, as the author of *Quo Vadis?*, a romance about the early Christians that I was never able to read. Like many other boys of my time, however—and apparently like Faulkner—I had been enthralled by his trilogy of patriotic novels based on Polish history: *With Fire and Sword, The Deluge,* and *Pan Michael.* They are in fact more than a trilogy; the Polish text was originally published in thirteen volumes, and the English translation in four thick, closely printed ones. I read them from beginning to end, even though I was a Northerner and did not draw the parallel that Faulkner must have drawn between the heroic but defeated past of Poland and that of the South.

It is more than a simple military parallel, for the life of the Polish gentry—with their habit of command, their fierce pride, their chivalric illusions, and their estates on the edge of a wilderness—bore an inescapable resemblance to the life of Mississippi planters before the Civil War. Among Sienkiewicz's heroes, it would be Pan Michael, "the little knight" who was the bravest swordsman in Poland, with whom Faulkner could most easily identify himself. But it is strange how his memory transformed the author's comment on his work. *Pan Michael* has no foreword. What Faulkner vividly but inaccurately remembered was the last sentence of the novel, which reads (in Jeremiah Curtin's translation): "Here ends this series of books, written in the course of a number of years and with no little toil, for the strengthening of men's hearts."

as to a novel—an entity of its own, single, set for one pitch, contrapuntal in integration, toward one end, one finale.

I think I have this one about right though you may not be familiar with all these pieces.

It is divided into sections, like this, with these section-designations:

I THE COUNTRY

Barn Burning
Shingles for the Lord
The Tall Men
A Bear Hunt
Two Soldiers

II THE VILLAGE

A Rose for Emily
Hair
Centaur in Brass
Dry September
Death Drag
Elly
Uncle Willy
Mule in the Yard
That Will Be Fine
That Evening Sun

III THE WILDERNESS

Red Leaves
A Justice

A Courtship
Lo!

IV THE WASTELAND

Ad Astra
Victory
Crevasse
Turnabout
All the Dead Pilots

V THE MIDDLE GROUND

Wash
Honor
Dr Martino
Fox Hunt
My Grandmother Millard
Golden Land
There Was a Queen
A Mountain Victory

VI BEYOND

Beyond
Black Music
The Leg
Mistral
Divorce in Naples
Carcassonne

I will write a foreword for it.
I went to Abercrombie and thought I had a corduroy coat

that would do but when I got home and looked at it,
it was wrong, too snappy, collegiate. I sent it back. I
still want one like yours, white or nearwhite corduroy,
bellows pockets and a loose belt and a vent in back so
I can ride a horse in it. Brooks said they had not had
them in two years. The next time you are in there, will
you see if they can get the corduroy and make me one
like yours?

My best most graceful remembrances to Muriel.

Bill F.

I answered the letter on the day it arrived.

November 3, 1948.

Dear Bill:

Sat up (or lay half-awake beside the radio) until four
o'clock listening to the election returns. I thought I
didn't give a damn about the election, but when the returns began to come in I found that I was still a Democrat
by inheritance if no other way, and really hated Mr.
Dewey, and I came downstairs this morning very sleepy
but with a grin. And, oh, what a joy it is to read the
names of all the bastards not re-elected to Congress.

The radio was still blaring at 11:30 when your letter
arrived and Mr. D had just sent his telegram of con-
gratulation to our dear little Harry, so that I first read
the letter with a rather absent eye. But I was, and on a
second reading am still more, delighted with your

arrangement of the short stories. Yes, it does the job
and does it well. Only one criticism, with which you
may not agree; I don't like to see the book ending with
the group of stories you call "Beyond," because they are
early work and were never my favorites—in fact this one
reader would be just as well pleased if you didn't
reprint them at all. But what I was going to suggest was
that you transpose the last two sections. "Beyond" comes
after "The Wasteland," in a way; and if you ended
with the group of stories in "The Middle Ground," you'd
be coming back closer to your general theme; and that
would make the book end with "A Mountain Victory,"
which is good and rounds off the story of The Man,
together with the Civil War story.

Ever think of writing a one- or two-page Epilogue?

It was fun for the family when an old lady from New
Milford drove up in a station wagon and tottered to
the door with a box containing a dozen roses (which she
had grown herself, incidentally). Muriel says they're
the first roses that anyone has sent her for years and
she's going to write thanking you.

I went out with my shotgun after you left and fired
it once in anger, but all I got was a red squirrel. The
ruffed grouse & pheasants had disappeared. I hope you get
at least a 12-point buck on your November trip.

As ever,

Malcolm

I still think my suggestion about transposing the last two sections of the *Collected Stories* was a good one, but Faulkner didn't accept it; in fact he didn't answer the letter. I was next to hear from him two months later and in connection with another subject, the profile for *Life*. Still later, when the *Collected Stories* appeared in 1950, I was to find that he had followed the table of contents given in his letter, except that he had included four more of his previously uncollected stories, "Shall Not Perish," "Pennsylvania Station," "Artist at Home," and "The Brooch," none of which is among his best. I would also find, somewhat to my disappointment, that he had abandoned the notion of writing a foreword. As a result of that decision, the theme on which a foreword might have been based, if he had written it, was available for future use.

It was of course the theme suggested by that phrase he remembered (and why not inaccurately, after so many years?) from his boyhood reading of *Pan Michael:* "travail (he may even have said agony and sacrifice) for the uplifting of men's hearts." I think—I am almost certain—that there are echoes of the phrase, both magnified and distant, like thunder among the hills, at the beginning and the end of Faulkner's Nobel Prize address. At the beginning he says, "I feel that this award was not made to me as a man but to my work—a life's work in the agony and sweat of the human spirit. . . ." Almost at the end he says that it is the writer's privilege "to help man endure by lifting his heart, by reminding him of the courage and honor and hope and pride and compassion and pity and sacrifice which have been the glory of his past."

VIII

Since there was another long essay that came earlier on my schedule, I had done no further work on the Faulkner profile. In my papers I find a list of "People to Consult" about him, but I hadn't yet consulted them; there was time. Then, soon after New Year's, Faulkner sent me a perturbed letter.

[Oxford] Wednesday. [January 5, 1949]

Dear Malcolm:

I have waited two weeks, and am still no nearer getting into the dentist's chair. About 10 years ago I had no little difficulty in convincing Life (or somebody) that I didn't want a piece about me in their mag. and two years ago it took six months and a considerable correspondence and telegrams to convince Vogue that I would have no part of their same project.

I still dont want it, I mean, me as a private individual, my past, my family, my house. I would prefer nothing about the books, but they are in the public domain and I was paid for that right. The only plan I can accept is one giving me the privilege of editing the result. Which means I will want to blue pencil everything which even intimates that something breathing and moving sat behind the typewriter which produced the books.

I imagine this wont go down with LIFE. I imagine the last thing on earth they will pay their good money for is a piece about somebody's mere output even though art, since I imagine they dont care two whoops in the bad place about art but only about what they would call 'personalities'. But I am still trying to think of some workable approach so you can collect on it. I haven't done it yet, since I cant know what or how much you can do keeping me out; that is, how much material suitable to Life will be left.

This is a damned bastardly clumsy letter. I'm trying to say No, but in a ten-page polysyllable since conscience, heart, liking and what dregs of gratitude I might possess, forbid that simple rapid word. Write me again, lets see if we cant work out something Life will take.

My best to Muriel.

Bill

RFD Gaylordsville, Conn.,
January 11, 1949.

Dear Bill:

I understand how you feel, or rather I don't understand but merely accept it as a looming fact of nature. Hadn't ever thought of doing a piece about you like the one on Hemingway, because I knew you didn't want that. [The piece had just appeared, in the January 10 issue of *Life*.] The pictures & captions that go with the Hemingway piece are pretty God-awful—I hadn't anything to do with them—but my part of it, the text, is straight and I think it's what Ernest wanted, once he had decided to let himself be profiled. The story is what he told me and what I learned about him—except for the things that might have made trouble for him, which I was careful to omit. I'll hear how he feels about it very shortly, having just mailed him the piece to his Italian hide-out; he had refused to see it before publication.

About you I had thought of doing another sort of piece entirely, taking the focus off Mr. Faulkner and putting it on Yoknapatawpha County. Assembling the county from its scattered pieces. Pictures, but not of the author— pictures of a house like the Old Frenchman's place, and of a black man plowing, and of an old church in the pine hills, and of a crossroads store on Saturday afternoon. There would have to be something about you in the piece, but I thought I could confine myself to what has been printed by or about you and is therefore public property.

That's what I thought, anyway, but your letter makes me stop to think again. Maybe we can still work on this angle or find another that wouldn't infringe on your privacy. It would have to be something that would make a good piece or it wouldn't be worth doing—and by a good piece I mean something interesting to write and useful to readers of your books. But if we can't use this angle or plot out another, I'll have to let it drop and with a hell of a lot of regret, because Messrs. Life & Co. would stake me to a trip to Mississippi and I would love to see you there, and they would pay a large round sum for the article, something I could use right now and feel happy about.

I had that trip marked out as something I'd like to do in early March, weather permitting. Would have to be back here March 16, because Rob comes home from school then and we haven't seen much of him since he started being a scholar.

You didn't say anything about the hunting trip—was it good? They've been jacking deer in these parts, where it's hard to shoot a deer legally—you have to get a special license countersigned by a special landowner and good only for his property. The valley has emptied, with all our friends wintering in NY or Italy or Mexico, and still I don't get much work done. You sound as if you were high, high on the wagon. I'm there too, with occasional lapses, because of the damnedest thing—indigestion which leaves me miserable for a week every time I spend an evening bending my elbow. I just finished reviewing Dos Passos' last novel [*The Grand Design*], which is terrible —disillusioned with everything he once admired and with everybody he used to like, and there have been great novels of disillusionment, like The Possessed, but it doesn't give Dos Passos an edge as it gave Dostoyevsky; it leaves him flat and trite and unable to feel anything about people except sometimes a dead pity and oftener a cold disgust.

As ever,
Malcolm

I wondered what Faulkner would say when he saw the Hemingway profile. It was, as I had told him, a straight-

forward account of Hemingway's career, about which I had
gathered a good deal of unfamiliar material; I was reason-
ably satisfied with what I had written. But the text was
surrounded, submerged, and, it seemed to me, changed in
import by a collection of intimate photographs, beginning
with a full-page portrait of Hemingway in his bedroom at
half-past six in the morning with five of his favorite cats: he
looms behind them, barefooted, bare-thighed, bare-chested,
while he meditatively sprinkles salt on his breakfast egg.
Other photographs were of Hemingway at the age of seven,
with his first fishing rod and an enormous creel; Hemingway at eight with a Buster Brown haircut, looking angelic
among his sisters; Hemingway wounded in World War I;
Hemingway gulping whisky from what I seem to remember
was the only bottle of White Horse in the Spanish Republican Army; Hemingway bespectacled and magnificently
bearded in an aviator's costume before flying a mission over
the German lines; and Hemingway's four wives, who, by an
inspiration of the make-up department, were candid-cam-
eraed on facing pages: look and compare. I was hardly
surprised by Faulkner's comment when it finally arrived.

Oxford, Friday. [February 11, 1949]

Dear Malcolm:

I saw the LIFE with your Hemingway piece. I didn't
read it but I know it's all right or you wouldn't have put
your name on it; for which reason I know Hemingway
thinks it's all right and I hope it will profit him—if there

is any profit or increase or increment that a brave man and an artist can lack or need or want.

But I am more convinced and determined than ever that this is not for me. I will protest to the last: no photographs, no recorded documents. It is my ambition to be, as a private individual, abolished and voided from history, leaving it markless, no refuse save the printed books; I wish I had had enough sense to see ahead thirty years ago and, like some of the Elizabethans, not signed them. It is my aim, and every effort bent, that the sum and history of my life, which in the same sentence is my obit and epitaph too, shall be them both: He made the books and he died.

But I still owe you a drunk. I will hold it on demand at sight draft, not transferable of course since you and Muriel will have to be present. But I will furnish someone to do the actual drinking; not myself this time.

Yours,

Bill

RFD Gaylordsville, Conn.,
February 17, 1949.

Dear Bill:

This winter I have a pheasant-feeding station outside my study window. I watch them when I ought to be writing. The hens are wild birds, hatched in these fields; they only come to the station very early in the morning and the least noise on the road sends them scurrying back among the pine trees. The cocks are state-raised birds, and although they got shot at last fall they have forgotten those unpleasant weeks and now act as if they owned the place. Just now, as I started to write you, a cock was trying to herd two frightened hens to the feed hopper, but they darted away and the cock after them. One cock roosts in my pine trees at night and talks to another cock in a swamp half a mile away. When I come out to saw wood just before sunset he raises a hell of a racket. "These are my trees," he seems to be saying, "you get to hell out of here."

I was in NY yesterday and had a long talk with Bob Coughlan of Life. He's the good guy on their staff. He felt very disappointed about your decision. He wanted me to make clear to you that the pictures with the Hemingway piece were taken by Ernest's consent, the big one by his own photographer, and were used with his permission. I said you'd like to know that but it wouldn't change your mind. We talked about the possibility I mentioned of doing a piece about your work without bringing you into it, but couldn't dredge up any possibilities. When "Intruder in the Dust" is filmed, the movie dept of Life wants to do scenes of the countryside, and that would obviously rule out the other idea I had.

Some time Life or another magazine—I can prophesy— is going to send a reporter to Oxford with instructions to get a story, and he'll do the job unscrupulously. That's the trouble with your decision—it's absolute for anyone who respects you and admires your work, but won't have any effect at all on the sons of bitches. I was thinking about it while watching the pheasants. My neighbor Ed Schimpf owns 250 acres and doesn't want any hunting on his land.

What he wants or doesn't want makes no difference at all
to the hunters who come up here from Danbury and
Bridgeport; out of my window in the fall I can watch them
moving across his fields—but being a neighbor of Ed's
and liking him, I can't follow them. I tell him he ought
to turn his rules upside down and let his neighbors shoot
when he knows they'll be careful, but bar out the Bridgeport
hunters who cut his fences.

I guessed from your last letters that you were either
writing hard or getting ready to write. I hope it's that way,
with the big book so far along. Have to report that the
Faulkner boom continues; some professors and librarians
told me in NY, over drinks, that your work was more
studied in the colleges than that of any other living
American author. . . .

As ever,

Malcolm

I didn't receive or expect a reply to the letter. By that
time I had learned that Faulkner didn't write me to offer
apologies or explain at greater length, but only when he had
something new to say. Also my guess was right that he was
again making progress on *A Fable,* after work on it had
been interrupted several times. "Well I am doing something
different now," he had said in a letter to Bob Linscott when
he started the novel, "so different that I am writing and
rewriting, weighing every word which I never did before.
I used to hang it on like an apprentice paper hanger and
never look back." Four years had passed since the letter

to Linscott, and he was still moving ahead slowly while weighing every word.

In November 1950 I wrote to congratulate him on the Nobel Prize. "The nice thing," I said, "was that everybody was pleased at your getting it. And it's wonderful that the Swedish Academy gave their prize this year to someone whose work really deserves it. . . . I wonder if you're making the hunting trip this fall. It's getting to be time for that —or will you surrender it for once and make the voyage to Stockholm?" Faulkner did make the hunting trip, as it turned out, and of course he also flew to Stockholm, after first refusing to go. It was not the Swedish ambassador or the State Department that changed his mind, but a plea from his daughter Jill, who wanted to go along. At last he said, "Every young girl ought to have a right to see Paris." An evening or two before they took the plane, Robert Haas gave another big dinner party, this time for the Nobel laureate and his daughter. Faulkner was polite but abstracted that evening, as if reserving his strength for a supreme ordeal. I thought he had the look to be found on the faces of British Tommies at Ypres, in photographs taken a moment before they went over the top. His eyes lighted only when he looked at Jill, who, shyly polite and self-possessed, was radiating the pleased excitement that her father might have been expected to feel.

After the Nobel Prize, *Life* was more than ever determined to have a profile of Faulkner, and another writer had undertaken to furnish it. Like other friends, apparently, I wrote to give warning of the project.

Sherman, Conn.,
May 20, 1951.

Dear Bill:

Last week in New York I had a call from a Life researcher named Mickie Murphy. She told me that Robert Coghlan of Life (I always forget just how he spells his name) was doing an article on you and she was doing the research for him and she wanted to talk to me about your work. I said I would see her when I got back to New York around the first of June.

Coghlan is an intelligent fellow and admires your work and probably his article won't be bad by the standard of Life close-ups—but that standard is a depressing one, as you know, and I'm glad that when there was talk of my doing one about you, you told me not to go ahead with it. I was sure then, however, that they would get someone else to do the job without your consent, and thought you ought to know about it. I'll talk to Miss Murphy about your work, but about nothing else.

Hope everything is going well. Muriel sends her love to you and yours.

As ever,

Malcolm

The profile, or "close-up," finally appeared in two installments, in the issues of *Life* dated October 5 and 12, 1953. It proved to be partly a description of Faulkner's mythical kingdom and partly a history of his family from 1839, the year when the first William Falkner arrived in Mississippi as a runaway boy of fourteen; both those topics were un-exceptionable. More of the article, however, consisted of anecdotes and conjectures about the author's private doings. Not being able to approach Faulkner himself or his immediate family or his editors or many of his close friends, the researchers for *Life* had looked for material wherever they could find it. Notably they had gone to Oxford and collected gossip about their subject as a local character who acted strangely at times and was said to drink a great deal of whisky. Everybody who knew Faulkner and read the article wondered what he would say about it.

Faulkner was spending the autumn in New York; he had a desk at Random House, where he was making final revisions on *A Fable*. It happened that I was present at what might have been a dramatic occasion: the first and, I believe, the only meeting between the author of the Faulkner profile and its subject. Not long after it appeared, Faulkner and I were having lunch with Bob Linscott and Saxe Commins at a restaurant around the corner from Random House. Linscott said, "There is Bob Coughlan over by the wall. Would you like to meet him?" Faulkner said, "I wouldn't mind." Linscott brought him over to our table and made the introductions; we all remained standing. Coughlan said embarrassedly that he was eager to know what Faulkner thought about his piece. There was a little breathless pause and then, "I haven't read it," Faulkner said easily, "but I'm sure it's all right." Coughlan said with more assurance that he had always deeply admired Faulkner's work. Faulkner thanked him politely but distantly, and a moment later Coughlan excused himself. There had been no drama.

Apparently Faulkner never got round to reading the profile or the short book into which Coughlan expanded it (*The Private World of William Faulkner;* Harper, 1954), but he was to hear about its contents from many sources. Later he expressed his feelings about it in a vehement article that was eventually published in the July 1955 issue of *Harper's* under the title "On Privacy—the American Dream: what happened to it." He is even more vehement, as well as being more specific, in a first draft of part of the article, a six-page manuscript that he gave to his friend Saxe Commins. By Mrs. Commins' very kind permission, I copy it here as a postscript to the whole episode.

FREEDOM: AMERICAN STYLE

About ten years ago Malcolm Cowley, a good friend of long standing, notified me that Life Magazine had offered him a good price to write a piece about me—not about my works, but about me as a private citizen, an individual. I said No, and explained why: my belief that only a writer's works were in the public domain, the writer himself having put them there by submitting them for publication and accepting money for them, and therefore he not only would but must accept whatever the public wished to think or say or do about them from praise to burning. But that, until the writer committed a crime or ran for public office, his private life was his own and not only had he the right to defend his privacy but the public had the duty to do so, since one man's liberty must stop

at exactly the point where the next one's begins; and that
I believed that anyone of taste and responsibility would
agree with me.

But Cowley said No. He said: 'You are wrong.
If I do the piece, I will do it with taste and responsibility.
But if you refuse me, sooner or later someone will do it
who will not bother about taste or responsibility either,
who will care nothing about you or your status as a
writer, an artist, but only as a commodity: merchandise:
to be sold, to increase circulation, to make a little money.'

'Nonsense,' I said. 'Until I commit a crime or announce
for office, they cant invade my privacy if I say No.'

'They not only can,' he said, 'but once your European
reputation gets back here and makes your coat-tails worth
riding, they will. Wait and see.'

Well, I did. Two years ago I learned by mere chance,
during a conversation with an editor in the house which
publishes my books, that the same magazine had already
set on foot the same project which I had declined; I dont
know whether the publishers were formally notified or if
they just heard about it by chance too, as I did. I said No
again, recapitulating the same reasons which I still believed
were not even arguable by anyone possessing the power of
the public press since the qualities of taste and responsibility
would have to be inherent in that power. The editor
interrupted.

'I agree with you,' he said. 'Besides, you dont need to
give reasons. The simple fact that you dont want it done
is enough. Shall I do it for you?' So he did, or tried it,
because my critic-friend was still right. Then I said,

'Try them again. Say "I ask you: please dont."' Then I submitted the same *I ask you: please dont,* the answer implying this time, as I recall: 'I've got to. If I refuse, they will fire me.' Which must be correct, since I got the same answer from the representative of another magazine on the same subject. So after that, if the writer, a member of the craft, was victim too of that facet of freedom, American style—that one calling itself Freedom of the Press—which I was victim of, the only defense left me was to refuse to co-operate, have anything to do with the project. Though even I realised by this time that that would do no good since at this point nothing I could do in life or death either would stop them.

And this time even I was right. Perhaps they—the writer and his employer—did not believe it; perhaps it is impossible for any American publisher or journalist to believe that any American (possibly anyone anywhere) except when he is hiding from the police, actually does not want his name and picture in the paper. Or perhaps they wanted me out of it since I would only have been in the way, insisting still on responsibility regarding the material even though I had already lost the battle regarding the bad taste of the invasion. (I did not read the articles; my information about them is hearsay, from my mother's shocked outrage and by telephone, telegraph and the Federal post from every male alcoholic in the United States; this day a year and they will all have phoned or wired or written, to move in and live with me: the unregenerate to help me drink it, the reformed to save me from it.)

So the writer with his party—group—crew (I dont know
how many; I never saw them) came (was sent; for his
sake I still prefer to believe that, victim too, he had no
choice either but to come and get his material where and
how he could—one of the party told my mother or
permitted her to assume an outright lie to persuade her
to be photographed—for the reason that he durst not return
empty-handed) and departed and published his articles.
Which is not the point. The point is not even that the
writer is not to be blamed for what he turned up with
since empty-handed he would have been fired from the
job which must be valuable to him even if it does seem
to have deprived him of the right to choose between good
and bad taste. It is not even that his employer is not to
blame since to hold his (the employer's) precarious own
in his precarious and towering craft like an inverted
pyramid balanced on its apex, which, like the man on the
tightrope, depends for balance, continuation, life itself
not on the compounding of mass but of speed, and which
in collapsing will destroy him too, he (the employer),
unless his is a really terrifying integrity, must serve the
time also.

The point is—the terrifying (not shocking; we should
not be shocked by it since we permitted its birth and
watched it grow and condoned and validated it and even
in individual cases use it at need) thing is—that it could
have happened at all, was possible to have happened at
all, its victim, even when accidentally warned in advance,
completely helpless to prevent it; nor, even after the fact,
without recourse since, unlike obscenity and degeneracy,

we have no laws against bad taste because unlike degeneracy
and obscenity we have not yet discovered how to sell bad
taste and know that's what we are selling; and even if there
were laws the publisher could charge the judgment and
court costs off income as operating loss, and the subsequent
profit from increased sales to capital investment. That in
America today any organization or group, simply by
functioning under a phrase like Freedom of the Press
or National Security or Anti-Subversion, can postulate for
itself complete immunity to violate the privacy of any
individual himself not a member of some federation
populous enough to frighten them off. Not artists of course;
being individuals, not even two of them could federate,
let alone enough; besides which, artists dont count in
America, there is no place for them, they have no more
business in American life than Life Magazine has in
Faulkner's. But the two other human occupations which
require privacy to endure, live, and which are valuable
to American life: science and humanity: the scientists and
the humanitarians—the pioneers in the science of endurance
and mechanical craftsmanship and self-discipline and skill
like Colonel Lindbergh compelled at last to repudiate
it by the harassment of that nation which arrogated to
itself the glory of his renown yet could neither protect
his children nor shield his grief; the pioneers in the
simple science of saving the nation like Doctor Oppenheimer,
harassed and impugned by that same nation until all
privacy was stripped from him and there remained only
the qualities of individualism whose possession we boast
since they alone differ us from animals—gratitude for

kindness, fidelity to friendship, chivalry toward women and the capacity to love—before which even his federated officially vetted harassers were impotent, turning away themselves (one hopes) in shame: as if the whole business had nothing whatever to do with loyalty or disloyalty but was simply to batter and strip him completely naked of the privacy lacking which he could never have become the individual capable of saving a nation at that moment when apparently nobody else was, and so reduce him at last to one more identityless integer in that identityless anonymous unprivacied mass which seems to be our goal.

The article as it finally appeared in *Harper's* is twice as long as this early draft and ends with a sustained philippic against the standards of the American press. Among other changes, my name disappears from the published text; I become "a well known literary critic and essayist," otherwise unidentified except as "a good friend of long standing." But Faulkner was speaking to me, in a sense, and I was grateful to him as for a personal letter—certainly not an apology, to which I had no shadow of a claim, but rather a simple acknowledgment that, if I had written the article, I might have betrayed the secret that there was a man sitting at Faulkner's typewriter, but still I would have presented him first and last as a man of letters, not as a magazine "personality."

IX

Faulkner had been a member of the National Institute of Arts and Letters since 1939. In the autumn of 1948 he was "elevated"—as William Dean Howells and his friends were fond of saying—to the American Academy, which might be called the senate of the Institute, limited as it is to fifty members chosen from all the arts. Each member has an armchair, as in the French Academy, and Faulkner was given Chair Four, which had first been occupied by the painter John La Farge.

When notified of the honor, he was very slow to reply. Felicia Geffen, the assistant to the president of the Academy, wrote him a rather plaintive letter at the end of December. She said, "On November 23, 1948, you were elected a member of the American Academy of Arts and Letters, and the President and the Secretary telegraphed and wrote you of your election. A Yearbook and Academy button were also sent to you at this time, and announcement was made in the New York newspapers, a clipping of which I enclose.

"We have never had any response from you, and the assumption is, of course, that you accept. I would appreciate so much having on file some word from you before the Academy Yearbook goes to press."

This time Faulkner answered immediately.

Oxford, Miss.
31 Dec. 1948.

Dear Sir:

The letter must have become mislaid after it reached my home, since I did not receive it. I was in a deer hunting camp Nov. 23. Telegrams are a casual business here; the office in town telephones them out and if you are not there to answer the phone, nothing else is done about it unless the operator happens to meet or pass you in the street and happens to remember to tell you a telegram came for you two or three weeks ago; did you get it?

I would have acknowledged otherwise, and take this opportunity to express my awareness of the honor.

Yours sincerely,

William Faulkner

There were other honors to come from the Academy. In the spring of 1950 he was chosen to receive the Howells Medal, which is given once every five years in recognition of the most distinguished work of American fiction published during that period. Technically Faulkner was being honored for his *Collected Stories,* which had just appeared, but of course the jury was thinking about the whole body of his work. When Mark Van Doren invited him to accept the medal at the Joint Ceremonial of the Institute and the Academy, to be held that year on May 25, Faulkner answered in his role of a Mississippi farmer.

Oxford, Miss.
1 April 1950

Dear Mr. Van Doren:

Thank you for your letter. I deeply appreciate this honor; nothing makes a man feel better than for his fellow craftsmen publicly and concretely to depose that his work is all right.

I would like to be present, of course. I am very sorry that right now I cant even say No. I am a farmer this time of year; up until he sells crops, no Mississippi farmer has the time or money either to travel anywhere on. Also, I doubt if I know anything worth talking two minutes about.

But you cant hang half fast and half loose just because I do, so perhaps the best is for me to say I will not be able to come up in May, and in great pride for the honor and gratitude for the letter, I am

Yours truly,

William Faulkner

After the Ceremonial, he received the Howells Medal by mail, together with a recording of the speech made by Archibald MacLeish when presenting it *in absentia*. Faulkner replied with a longer letter of acknowledgment.

Oxford, Miss.
12 June 1950

Secretary, American Academy,
New York.
Dear Sir:

The medal received, also the transcription of Mr. MacLeish. It's very fine indeed to have these concrete evidences—the gold and the voice—of the considered judgment of one's peers. A man works for a fairly simple —limited—range of things: money, women, glory; all nice to have, but glory's best, and the best of glory is from his peers, like the soldier who has the good opinion not of man but of other soldiers, themselves experts in it, who are themselves brave too.

Though it still seems to me impossible to evaluate a man's work. None of mine ever quite suited me, each time I wrote the last word I would think, if I could just do it over, I would do it better, maybe even right. But I was too busy; there was always another one. I would tell myself, maybe I'm too young or too busy to decide; when I reach fifty, I will be able to decide how good or not. Then one day I was fifty and I looked back at it, and I decided that it was all pretty good—and then in the same instant I realised that that was the worst of all since that meant only that a little nearer now was the moment, instant, night: dark: sleep: when I would put it all away forever that I anguished and sweated over, and it would never trouble me anymore.

William Faulkner

My own correspondence with Faulkner had languished, though I saw him occasionally in New York and had news of him from various parts of the world; that was the era of his travels for the State Department. In 1957 he was Writer in Residence at the University of Virginia. I was then serving as president of the National Institute, and I wrote him on Institute letterhead to ask a special favor.

March 2, 1957.

Dear Bill,

I wonder whether you could do a little chore this year for the Academy and the Institute. I don't think those august bodies have bothered you in the past, but this is a rather special occasion.

This year Dos Passos is being awarded the Gold Medal of the Institute for Fiction. It is almost the highest honor that we award (the only higher one being the Howells Medal, which you received in 1950). Presentation is made by a member of the Academy at the annual Ceremonial, which takes place I think on Wednesday May 22.

I was very pleased when the medal went to Dos Passos, because in recent years his work hasn't been sufficiently recognized—but that's a formal and lukewarm way of putting it; the truth is that he's had to stand up under an intermittent hail of brickbats. Of course his recent work hasn't been up to the level of what he did in the twenties and thirties, but he did a lot then; he took chances; he put other novelists in his lasting debt. And now that

he's being given a medal—the first, he says, since he was
a boy in school—I'd like to see the occasion made just as
big as possible, so that he knows the rest of us haven't
forgotten him.

That's why I'm asking whether, as the most distinguished
novelist in the Academy, you couldn't make the
presentation of the medal. It's not a big chore; about
two hundred words would be all that would be required,
though of course you'd have to start by being present
that afternoon,—but that wouldn't be too painful, because
it's a pleasant occasion, with good food, drink, and
conversation before we go to the platform, to sit there for
an hour and a half.

But I'd better stop urging and leave it up to you, with
one other request. If you can't come, as may well prove
to be the case, will you drop me a line fast, so that we can
make some other arrangement?

As ever,
Malcolm

I was surprised by his answer, which arrived promptly.

[No date]

Dear Malcolm:

I hate like bejesus to face this sort of thing, but maybe
when his vocation has been as kind to a bloke as this one
has been to me, an obligation such as this is a part of the

bloke's responsibility toward it. So, if you are sure I am the man, I will take on the job and do the best I know.

Let me know the date exactly.

Bill

c/o Department of English,
University of Virginia,
Charlottesville, Va.

I wrote to give more details of what the job would be, and Faulkner appeared for the Ceremonial on the morning of May 22.

The Joint Ceremonial of the Institute and the Academy, held in the Academy building, is the occasion for a combined prize day, spring festival of the arts, and tribal corroboree. For members and their wives or husbands, the day starts with a reading of tributes to deceased academicians. Then comes a cocktail hour, then a luncheon party at big round tables, all humming with conversation; then the members gather in the Dodd Room, or greenroom, before taking their places on the stage. Facing a crowded auditorium, they proceed to the business of the afternoon: new members of the Academy and the Institute are formally inducted, grants and medals are conferred, and an invited speaker delivers the annual Blashfield Address. Afterward the audience inches its way upstairs, through narrow corridors, to an art exhibition in the gallery and a huge reception on the terrace.

Faulkner couldn't be happy on such an occasion, but he did his best to act like a good student on commencement day. Halfway through the luncheon the two of us were called into another room, with Dos Passos, to rehearse the presentation for the benefit of photographers. I have one of the shots they took: it shows Faulkner erect and abstracted, holding out the medal, while Dos Passos beams through his spectacles as he reaches out for it with a hand that came too close to the camera and looks enormous. The rehearsal had scarcely ended when the members were summoned to the greenroom and the stage. The organ began to play.

It was Faulkner's first Ceremonial, and unfortunately it lasted a little longer than the others. There seemed to be more citations to read and more grants to be conferred as their recipients came up from the audience to shake hands with the president of the Institute. The Blashfield Address, delivered that year by Salvador de Madariaga, was short in reality, but it seemed interminable. Faulkner's presentation of the Gold Medal had been placed late on the program. Twice, I think it was, he left the stage and went down to the greenroom for a smoke. Finding a secretary there, he asked, "How long does *this* go on?" He unfolded the sheet of paper on which his speech had been typed. Later it was printed in the *Proceedings* of the Academy.

The artist, the writer [he was to have said], must never have any doubts about where he intends to go; the aim, the dream, must be that high to be worth that destination and the anguish of the effort to reach it. But he must have humility regarding his competence to get there, about his craft and his craftsmanship in it.

So the fact that the artist has no more actual place in the American culture of today than he has in the American economy of today, no place at all in the warp and woof, the thews and sinews, the mosaic of the American dream as it exists today, is perhaps a good thing for him, since it teaches him humility in advance, gets him into the habit of humility well ahead whether he would or no; in which case, none of us has been better trained in humility than this man whom the Academy is honoring today. Which proves also that that man, that artist, who can accept the humility, will, must, in time, sooner or later, work through the humility and the oblivion into that moment when he and the value of his life's work will be recognized and honored at least by his fellow craftsmen, as John Dos Passos and his life's work are at this moment.

It is my honor to share in his by having been chosen to hand this medal to him. No man deserves it more, and few have waited longer for it.

It was a good speech, written with some anguish of spirit and also, I think, with the notion of repaying the small but real debt to Dos Passos that he owed from his early years. It was not, however, to be delivered that afternoon. Appalled by hearing so many words, Faulkner decided to make his own sacrifice to the public interest and the cause of brevity. His trips to the greenroom had been an opportunity to strip off the less essential parts of his speech, sentence by sentence, as if he were husking an ear of corn. When he finally presented the medal to Dos Passos, he spoke a very few words that no one on the stage could hear. The legend among members of the Institute is that he said, "Here it is, Dos. Take it." But his actual words have been recorded and, though brief, they were much more dignified. "Oratory," he said, "can't add anything to John Dos Passos' stature,

and if I know anything about writers"—himself included—
"he may be grateful for a little less of it. So I'll say, mine is
the honor to partake of his in handing this medal to him.
No man deserves it more."

Faulkner himself received the Gold Medal for Fiction
the next time it was awarded, in 1962. The delay in his case
was due to an argument in the Council of the Institute over
two related questions. First, which was the greater honor,
the Howells Medal, which Faulkner had already received,
or the Gold Medal for Fiction? It was a long discussion, but
the Gold Medal carried the day. Second, could both medals
be awarded, in the course of time, to the same author?
Someone discovered a precedent—Willa Cather had received
both of them—and thereby cleared the way to putting Faulkner's name on the ballot that was sent to the membership.
Two or three other distinguished novelists were named on
the same ballot, but nobody questioned what the result of
the vote would be.

Faulkner, who was by then established in Charlottesville,
wrote that he would accept the medal at the Ceremonial
on May 24.

As the day approached, there were doubts expressed about
whether he would appear. The members should have known
that he had a habit of keeping his word. On April 29, however, President Kennedy had given a dinner at the White
House for the Nobel laureates; forty-nine of them had attended it, and Faulkner wasn't among them. When asked
why he had declined the presidential invitation, he answered,

according to the *New York Times,* "Why, that's a hundred miles away. That's a long way to go just to eat." New York was a much longer way, and the trip would be just to collect a medal which, if he didn't come to get it, would later arrive in the mail. But Faulkner set a higher value on awards from his fellow craftsmen than he did on official honors.

During the cocktail hour before the Ceremonial, my wife found him standing alone, as if surrounded by a ring of silence in that jolly bedlam. She introduced him to dozens of people, many of whom, including Conrad Aiken, he had surely met before. Faulkner recited a poem of Aiken's that he had memorized in his early years. At luncheon Muriel sat at his right, with Kenneth Burke at her other side. Trying to enlist Faulkner in small talk across the big round table merely resulted in silences, for any threat of social involvement made him retire into himself. He exchanged sporadic remarks with the Burkes, but it wasn't until he began to talk of riding to hounds through the Virginia countryside and of how he enjoyed living in Charlottesville near his adored daughter and her three little boys that he began to relax. He wanted a granddaughter too—"Little girls are born civilized," he said. Muriel assured him that granddaughters could be as noisy, scampish, wild, and adventuresome as little boys. Then Faulkner talked about the trip to Oxford he was planning to make in a pick-up truck; he chuckled at the idea. That day he had a country look, his face bronzed under the white hair and apparently glowing with health. As Muriel wrote to a friend, his magnificent dark eyes had the clarity that young children's often have.

Again there was the business of being called away from

dessert to be photographed, and again there was the summons to the stage. This time, however, the presentation of the Gold Medal had been placed very early in the program, so that Faulkner wouldn't get tired of hearing other people's words before speaking his own. Eudora Welty made the presentation, in a speech that was written and delivered with honest feeling. Faulkner's acceptance—which was the last public statement of his career—had a tone of retrospection, of lament for the dignity and freedom of the past, that was not exactly new for him, but that seemed to have a new resonance. He compared his own gold medal with those that used to be awarded to products displayed at Leipzig, St. Louis, and other world's fairs.

I think that those gold medals [he said in part], royal and unique above the myriad spawn of their progeny which were the shining ribbons fluttering and flashing among the booths and stalls of forgotten county fairs in recognition and accolade of a piece of tatting or an apple pie, did much more than record a victory. They affirmed the premise that there are no degrees of best; that one man's best is the equal of any other best, no matter how asunder in time or space or comparison, and should be honored as such.

We should keep that quantity, more than ever now, when roads get shorter and easier between aim and gain and goals become less demanding and more easily attained, and there is less and less space between elbows and more and more pressure on the individual to relinquish into one faceless serration like a mouthful of teeth, simply in order to find room to breathe. We should remember those times when the idea of an individuality of excellence compounded of resourcefulness and independence and uniqueness not only deserved a blue ribbon but got one.

Let the past abolish the past when—and if—it can substitute something better; not us to abolish the past simply because it was.

After all the grants and medals had been conferred, we found him sitting on a bench in the hallway, once more surrounded with a ring of silence. We asked him whether he would like us to drive him downtown, but he thanked us and said no; he had promised to wait there for Donald Klopfer of Random House. In the bustle of members looking for their hats, he seemed very much alone.

Six weeks later we heard over the radio that he had died suddenly in Oxford.

X

Long after the shock of Faulkner's death, I found myself looking back at him not only with the old admiration for his work but with respect for his character and also, it seems to me, with a degree of understanding. For all the differences between us, of which the enormous one was his genius, we were men of the same time, with many of the same standards, which were partly derived from our reading of the same authors, and we had the same instinctive love of the American land. His actions did not seem inexplicable to me, as they sometimes did to others. They were his own solutions, fresh and simple ones, as if he were acting without precedents, to problems that almost all the writers of our time had to face.

We were most of us countrymen, in one sense or another. There were exceptions and Scott Fitzgerald, for example, was less at home in the country, "up to my ass in daisies," than he was in a residential suburb. Most of the others lived in the country by choice, though preferably not too far from New York or Paris or, in Hemingway's case, Havana; or they found another compromise, as Cummings did by spending seven or eight months of the year in New York and the rest of it on a hilltop in New Hampshire. Perhaps we might be called a transitional generation, bent on enjoying the urban pleasures, but at the same time hunters and fishermen eager to feel the soil instead of asphalt underfoot. We were radicals in literature and sometimes in politics, but conservative in our other aspirations, looking back for ideals to the country we had known in childhood, where people led separate lives in widely scattered houses; where there were broad fields in which a boy could hunt without fear of No Trespass signs, and big woods, untouched by lumbermen, in which he could wander with a pocket compass. I suspect that we were the last generation in which those country tastes could be taken for granted. American fiction and poetry since our time have become increasingly urban or suburban.

Among us Faulkner was the only one who remained loyal to the neighborhood he had always known. The rest of us were uprooted and exiled from our native countrysides, at first by our schooling, then by the Great War, then by our travels; as one after another said, but Hemingway long before Wolfe, "You can't go home again." Faulkner seemed to be unaffected by that long deracination, as by the effort that followed it to put down new roots in middle age. He spent most of his life in Oxford, the country town where he grew up, which is thirty miles as the crow flies from New Albany, the other country town where he was born. He was nourished on local tradition and expressed it in his books: what was best in it as well as what was most violent and ominous. Yet there was another sense in which he too was uprooted; in which he lived as a foreigner among his neighbors and—to use a phrase that goes back to the Hitler era—an "internal émigré." For of course he lived almost from boyhood by another system of values—shared by many writers of his time—as well as by the local one; I mean the values of the artist in the Symbolist tradition.

The wonder is that he learned about that international tradition at such an early age, and in Oxford. He was introduced to it by a course of reading that started before his seventeenth birthday. In the summer of 1914 his neighbor Phil Stone came back from Yale. Faulkner "was painting some then," Stone said in a reminiscence printed in the Oxford weekly newspaper, the *Eagle*,[1] "and was faintly interested in writing verse. I gave him books to read— Swinburne, Keats and a number of the moderns, such as Conrad Aiken and the Imagists in verse and Sherwood Anderson in prose." I doubt whether anyone else in Oxford had those books at the time, except for Keats and Swinburne, but the list sounds familiar to me, since I was reading the same authors then or a little later, after the same sort of introduction by an older friend. And of course I went on, as Faulkner obviously did, to read others more definitely in the Symbolist tradition: Flaubert, Baudelaire, Verlaine, Rimbaud, Eliot, Joyce.

Faulkner was always a great reader, as one discovered in the course of time. Apparently he read poetry admired by the Symbolists, then fiction in the same tradition (though he would read almost any novel if it was recommended by people he respected or was written by one of his rivals), then Southern history and books about the Indians, and always Shakespeare and the Bible. He did not read the

---

[1] In the issue of November 14, 1950, after the announcement that Faulkner had been awarded the Nobel Prize.

moral or social philosophers of our time, but there was in fact a great deal of disguised ethics, with a touch of metaphysics, in the Symbolist poets and novelists, who had founded what has often been called a religion of art. Faulkner seems to have found the religion congenial, for he was always a moralist, by one system of values or another.

In his later years the system was essentially Christian. In his early books, however—and to some extent in the later ones as well—he applied the Symbolist precepts, including the simple one that actions should be judged as art. Instead of being extolled or condemned for their social consequences, they should be observed and presented for their dramatic qualities. The most reprehensible actions, in social terms, might be precisely those which enhanced a work of art by virtue of their passion and singlemindedness, or "purity." That would explain why Faulkner showed something close to admiration for most of his villains, including Jason Compson, Joe Christmas (if he *is* a villain), and Mink Snopes, and why, if he returned to them in his later writing—as he returned to Jason in the Appendix on the Compson family and to Mink in the best chapters of *The Mansion*—he presented them almost with affection. Even Mink's rich cousin Flem, the type of everything that Faulkner detested, acquires a redeeming dignity at the end. It was as if the author felt that he owed a debt to those characters for lending strength to his work.

It was the work, not the author, that was important by the Symbolist system of values. The author should sacrifice himself to the work, producing it "in the agony and sweat of the human spirit," as Faulkner said, "not for glory and least of all for profit, but to create out of the materials of the human spirit something which did not exist before." Since he was sacrificing himself, he might claim the right to sacrifice others. "An artist," Faulkner told Jean Stein when she interviewed him for the *Paris Review,* ". . . is completely amoral in that he will rob, borrow, beg, or steal from anybody and everybody to get the work done. . . . Everything goes by the board: honor, pride, decency, security, happiness, all, to get the book written." To produce the work was the categorical imperative, and it was combined for many Symbolists—as it was for Faulkner—with the metaphysical notion of soaring in the work toward an unchanging realm of passions transmuted into art, a sort of heaven for good books where they dwell in timeless equality. One remembers the letter in which he said, "All the moving things are eternal in man's history and have been written before, and if a man writes hard enough, sincerely enough, humbly enough, and with the unalterable determination never never never to be quite satisfied with it, he will repeat them, because art like poverty takes care of its own."

The Symbolist movement was not only a religion with saints and martyrs; it was also a sort of international freemasonry (of the French or Grand Orient rather than the Scottish Rite). Many of its moral precepts proved somewhat confusing to the uninitiated. Note for example the general reaction to Faulkner's statement, in his introduction to the Modern Library edition of *Sanctuary,* that the book "was deliberately conceived to make money."

I decided [he says] I might just as well make some of it myself. I took a little time out, and speculated what a person in Mississippi would believe to be current trends, chose what I thought was the right answer and invented the most horrific tale I could imagine and wrote it in about three weeks and sent it to [Harrison] Smith, who had done *The Sound and the Fury* and who wrote me immediately, "Good God, I can't publish this. We'd both be in jail." So I told Faulkner, "You're damned. You'll have to work now and then for the rest of your life."

That was enough to persuade most critics, at the time, that the book must be valueless and that Faulkner had degraded himself by committing an aesthetic crime. They scarcely bothered to read his qualifying statement that, after *Sanctuary* had at last been set into type, "I tore the galleys down and rewrote the book. It had already been set up once, so I had to pay for the privilege of rewriting it, trying to make out of it something which would not shame *The Sound and the Fury* and *As I Lay Dying* too much and I made a fair job. . . . " But Faulkner's writing contemporaries read the whole introduction, and most of them were more favorably impressed by it than the critics had been (while noting its disastrous effect on the public). They had learned by experience that the Muses are capricious, and it seemed to them—even before reading the book—that something written and revised in that fashion might prove to be an accidental masterpiece (as is indeed the case with *Sanctuary*). They did not feel that Faulkner had transgressed the laws of their profession by writing a book at top speed simply to make money. What he did was "all right," they said to themselves, provided that it was strictly an experiment and provided that his subsequent books were also experiments, but of different natures. It was writing another book by the same formula—something he never did—that would have been a sin against the religion of art.

Moreover—I am trying to depict a state of mind that I more or less shared at the time—there was something bold and grandly disdainful in the whole project. To speculate about current tastes; to meet them by inventing the most horrific tale that could be imagined, then by writing it in three weeks; to find after some delay that one's answer had been correct and was to be rewarded with almost as much money as one had dreamed of making; and later, when the book was reissued, to write an introduction that revealed the process offhandedly—all that showed an admirable independence of mind, as well as a vast indifference to what the public might think. As if by sure instinct, Faulkner was obeying another moral precept of the Symbolists: that the author should *épater les bourgeois*—not "shock the bourgeois," as the phrase is usually translated, but startle and affront respectable people, quite literally, knock them off their pins. He should do so with a negligent air, as if drawing on his gloves, and then, never repeating himself, he should move on to some new exploit or experiment.

Those were some rules of literary conduct, a few among others, that we learned in our time and more or less tried to follow. Because of our travels, most of us had the advantage of learning them in Paris from the best instructors. Faulkner stayed at home, except for his two or three years in New Orleans, and nevertheless he outdid the rest of us; he simply *was* what we vaguely thought of becoming. That is one reason—though his work is the principal reason—why he was admired by writers of his own generation at a time when his books as well as his actions confused the American public.

Even when his reputation was in eclipse, almost everyone was willing to grant that he had genius. Not so widely recognized then or later was that he also had talent. Here I am using the two words in one of their several pairings, one by which they are not measured on the same quantitative scale —with 180, for example, as a quotient for genius and 150 for talent—but instead are treated as sharply opposing qualities. "Genius" in that sense would stand for everything that is essentially the gift of the subconscious mind—inspiration, imagination, the creative vision—while "talent" would stand for conscious ingenuity, calculation, acquired skill, and the critical judgment that an author displays when revising his own work. "How many young geniuses we have known," Emerson said, "and none but ourselves will ever hear of them for want in them of a little talent."

Faulkner had talent in abundance, as is clear to anyone who examines the early draft of *Sanctuary,* for instance, or his three successive versions of "That Evening Sun." Each of his many changes reveals a sound critical judgment. The detective stories he collected in *Knight's Gambit* are examples of misapplied but impressive ingenuity. Again it was talent, not genius, that he revealed while working in Hollywood. He said in the *Paris Review* interview (1956), "I know now that I will never be a good motion-picture writer," but what he meant is that he wouldn't be a great one. He was good enough so that Warner Brothers made strenuous efforts to get him back to their studio, even in the years before they realized that he was a world-famous author. They wanted him because he could throw away the script and write new dialogue on the set, a technical achievement that few of their writers had mastered. But technique was never what excited him, and very often, I think, he sacrificed his talent to his genius.

The sacrifice is revealed not only in his books but in many casual remarks like those he made to me in Sherman. "I listen to the voices, and when I put down what the voices say, it's right. Sometimes I don't like what they say"—that is, their message might be in conflict with his conscious standards—"but I don't change it." Or that other remark, also quoted in an earlier chapter, "Get it down. Take chances," that is, give rein to the unconscious. "It may be bad, but that's the only way you can do anything really good. Wolfe took the most chances, though he didn't always know what he was doing. I come next and then Dos Passos. Hemingway doesn't take chances enough."

That was the argument at a distance between Faulkner and Hemingway, which sometimes became embittered on Hemingway's part. They had to differ, for the simple reason that they were rivals who—partly by the influence on both of them of their time—resembled each other in many fashions, great and small. Both of them had sharp eyes for landscape; both liked to go barefoot as boys and even as young men, as if they weren't satisfied with merely seeing the countryside but had to feel it as well; both were hunters by devoted avocation. Both loved the wilderness, lamented its passing, went searching for remains of it, and were proud of their ability to find their way in it without guides. Both returned in their work to many of the same themes: for example, the primitive mind, the mystical union of hunter and hunted, the obsessions of wounded men, and the praise of alcohol. There were even trivial resemblances, as in the British style of dress and the British officer's World War I mustache that Hemingway wore in his early years and Faulkner all his life. They differed radically, however, in their attitude toward the craft of writing.

Hemingway kept his inspiration in check, for he liked to know what he was doing at every moment. Quite the opposite of Faulkner in this respect, he sometimes sacrificed his genius to his talent. One thinks of his remark that I repeated in a letter: "Faulkner has the most talent of anybody"—here "talent" is being used in a different sense from mine—"but hard to depend on because he goes on writing after he is tired and seems as though he never threw away the worthless. I would have been happy just to have managed him." Hemingway was an excellent manager of others, and of himself until the last years, but it seems to me that he was wrong in this instance. The crucial problem with Faulkner was not that of managing his talent—let us say, of developing his skill and conserving his stamina as if he were a boxer training for the big fight—but rather that of keeping his genius alive through the years. To that problem he had to find his own solution.

All his life Faulkner was a problem solver. Obviously that was the way his mind worked: he regarded each new situation as a problem, which he usually reduced to a single question; then he tried to find his answer. It is of course a common procedure, but most of us make it easier by looking for precedents and then by responding to the problem with some action of which we hope the neighbors will say, "It's what any sensible person would have done in his case." Faulkner was not concerned with what his sensible neighbors might have done. He approached each problem as if nobody else had ever been faced with it and as if it required some radically new solution. In that respect he preserved a sort of innocence, a quality of mind or character that makes one think of the youngest son in fairy tales. Always the older brothers believe that the youngest is hopelessly stupid and ignorant of the world, but always he performs the right actions out of sheer simplicity.

So it is in the tale of "The Youth Who Went Forth to Learn What Fear Was." His quest leads him into a haunted castle where anyone who spends three nights will be rewarded with an immense treasure. Nobody else has come out alive after the first night, but the youth survives till morning by finding the proper answers. Then on the second night (I quote from the Brothers Grimm),

he again went up into the old castle, sat down by the fire, and once more began his old song: "If I could but shudder!" When midnight came, an uproar and noise of tumbling about was heard; at first it was low, but it grew louder and louder. Then it was quiet for a while, and at length with a loud scream, half a man came down the chimney and fell before him.

"Hullo!" cried the youth [as Faulkner might have cried]. "Another half belongs to this. This is not enough."

Then the uproar began again, there was a roaring and howling, and the other half fell down likewise. "Wait," said he, "I will just stoke up the fire a little for you." When he had done that and looked round again, the two pieces were joined together and a hideous man was sitting in his place.

"That is no part of our bargain," said the youth. "The bench is mine." The man wanted to push him away. The youth, however, would not allow that, but thrust him off with all his strength, and seated himself again in his own place.

Problem: What do you do when two halves of a body fall down the chimney, when they join together into a hideous man, and when he takes your place by the fire? Why, nothing could be simpler: you push him off the bench. *Problem that follows:* What do you do when other men fall down the chimney, bringing with them two skulls and nine thighbones of dead men, then stand up the bones and start playing ninepins with the skulls? Why, nothing could be simpler, considering that you had the foresight to provide yourself with a turning lathe. You grind the skulls till they are round and then join happily in the game. *Problem* (this time in Faulkner's terms): What do you do when you find yourself at a grisly Hollywood party, with guests more fearsome to you than specters in a haunted castle, but when you don't want to embarrass the host by making public excuses for leaving? Why, nothing could be simpler. You go upstairs, open a window, and escape by climbing down a trellis (while probably thinking of Miss Quentin Compson and her escape down a rainspout—or was it a pear tree?).

And still another problem solved in Faulkner's terms: A motion-picture studio has put him on its payroll, but without telling him what to do. He simply waits in Oxford for instructions. Then a telegram arrives: WILLIAM FAULKNER, OXFORD, MISS. WHERE ARE YOU? MGM STUDIO. As he later told Jean Stein when being interviewed:

I wrote out a telegram: MGM STUDIO, CULVER CITY, CALIF. WILLIAM FAULKNER.

The young lady operator said, "Where is the message, Mr. Faulkner?" I said, "That's it." She said, "The rule book says that I can't send it without a message, you have to say something." So we went through her samples and selected I forget which one—one of the canned anniversary messages. I sent that.

Those pleasant anecdotes reveal a pattern that Faulkner also followed, or tells us he followed, in writing his novels: always there was the problem reduced to a simple question, and always there was the simple but unprecedented answer. In *Sanctuary,* as we have seen, the problem was chiefly that of making money, and the answer was to invent "the most horrific tale I could imagine." In *As I Lay Dying,* the problem was what an imagined group of people would do when subjected to "the simple universal natural catastrophes, which are flood and fire, with a simple natural motive to give direction to their progress." The answer in the writing of the novel "was not easy. No honest work is. It was simple in that all the material was already at hand. It took me just about six weeks in the spare time from a twelve-hour-a-day job at manual labor." The problem was never the same. In *The Sound and the Fury*—as Faulkner tells us in a passage already quoted—it was presented by an obsessive mental picture: "the muddy seat of a little girl's drawers in a pear tree, where she could see through a window where her grandmother's funeral was taking place and report what was happening to her brothers on the ground below." But who were the children, what were they doing, and why were her pants muddy? By the time those questions were answered in his mind, Faulkner "realized it would be impossible to get all of it into a short story and that it would have to be a book." *The Wild Palms,* though it ended as a novel with two plots told in alternating chapters, started, so he explains, as the simple story of two people "who sacrificed everything for love, and then lost that." The question was how to keep the story at a high pitch of intensity.

When I reached the end of what is now the first section of *The Wild Palms* [he told Jean Stein], I realized suddenly that something was missing, it needed emphasis, something to lift it like counterpoint in music. So I wrote on the "Old Man" story until "The Wild Palms" story rose back to pitch. Then I stopped the "Old Man" story at what is now its first section, and took up "The Wild Palms" story until it began again to sag. Then I raised it to pitch again with another section of its antithesis, which is the story of a man who got his love and spent the rest of the book fleeing from it, even to the extent of voluntarily going back to jail where he would be safe.

As he explains the writing of each novel, he makes it sound as innocent as the behavior of the youth in the haunted castle. Faulkner too was exorcising demons and specters, but that seemed to be a trifling matter for a man who couldn't shudder. All he had to do, apparently, was to resolve each threatening situation into a question that could be answered in its own terms. We say once more, "Why, nothing could be simpler," and then with a start we realize that the questions were new and that the answers in each case were those of genius.

There were continuing problems in life to which he applied the same pattern of response. Of course the great problem of his early years was one that perplexes almost every young writer: how to live while getting his work done. Without reading Thoreau, it would seem, he instinctively chose Thoreau's answer: "Simplify, simplify!" He reduced his needs to the requisites of the writer's trade, which are, as he listed them to Jean Stein, "whatever peace, whatever solitude, and whatever pleasure he can get at not too high a cost," and beyond these, "Paper, tobacco, food, and a little whisky." The requisites could be supplied by any sort of odd job that was locally available, including house painting, rum running (from New Orleans), and shoveling coal in the University of Mississippi power station—always provided that the job didn't engross his attention and that he didn't hold it beyond the point of utter boredom.

That sort of barefoot heedlessness couldn't last after his marriage in 1929; his income as a family man had to be less intermittent. For a few years after *Sanctuary* (1931), his books and magazine stories produced enough to support the household. Then, in the later years of the depression, he found another expedient, which was to work in Hollywood for six months of the year and, by frugal living, to save enough from his never brilliant salary to carry him through the next six months in Oxford. Though not a happy answer, it was the best to be found.

But other problems remained, among them the one which I said was really crucial and which persisted from the years of obscurity into those of fame, that is, the problem of keeping his genius alive in a generally hostile environment. Faulkner's genius was essentially his sustained power of imagination. It could not be locked in a vault like precious stones; it needed space and air and especially solitude in which to breathe and grow. In my introduction to the Portable I had suggested that intellectual solitude was responsible for the faults in his writing (and Faulkner had agreed with me), but I should have seen even then that it was also a precondition of his writing. Only in solitude could he enter the inner kingdom—"William Faulkner, sole owner and proprietor"—that his genius was able to people and cultivate. Only by standing guard at the borders of the kingdom could he bar out invaders who might lay it waste. And that was only part of his guardianship, for he also had to be vigilant against tempters and corrupters who might destroy it from within.

His struggle against those two dangers was more precarious and his measure of victory over them was more admirable than is generally recognized. What we forget is that Faulkner was the first distinguished American man of letters who spent most of his life in a country town remote from any metropolitan center. Concord, of course, was also a country town, and the fact might help to explain some curious points of resemblance between Faulkner and the

Concord sages, especially Hawthorne. There was also Emerson, who said in one of his journals—as Faulkner might have echoed—"Alone is wisdom. Alone is happiness. Society nowadays makes us low spirited, hopeless. Alone is heaven." But when Emerson got tired of being alone in heaven, he had literary neighbors for distraction, and Concord in his time was only an hour on the cars from Boston. For Thoreau it was a half-day's walk from the Harvard Library. So, Concord is no exception to my generality, and neither is the fact that a few gifted women had survived as writers in towns no larger than Oxford; one thinks first of Emily Dickinson, then of Mary Noailles Murfree and Elizabeth Madox Roberts. A gentlewoman's problem was slightly different in a country town, that is, if she didn't marry; she was permitted by public opinion, she might even be encouraged, to spend her leisure writing books instead of painting china. A man, however, was expected to follow some practical pursuit like farming or merchandising or legal counseling, at the cost, if he failed to do so, of being ridiculed as "Count No'count" by his former classmates. Perhaps that weight of public ridicule and incomprehension has been the greatest enemy of the arts in rural America. Faulkner was by no means the first man to resist it, but he was the first not to be warped by his resistance; the first simply to stand his ground and pursue a fruitful literary career.

To do so required pride, will power, and tough-hided indifference, in a measure of all three that is not generally associated with an imaginative writer. Moreover, he also had to display those qualities on another battlefield. When he emerged from his country town, as he did for as much as six months of the year, it was to work in Hollywood, which used to have a notorious fashion of embracing and destroying men of letters. After publishing an admired book, or two or three, the writer was offered a contract by a movie studio; then he bought a house with a swimming pool and vanished from print. If he reappeared years later, it was usually with a novel designed to have the deceptive appeal of an uplift brassière. The process aroused Faulkner's scorn. "Nothing can injure a man's writing," he told Jean Stein, "if he's a first-rate writer. . . . The problem does not apply if he is not first rate, because he has already sold his soul for a swimming pool." Faulkner protected his soul, or rather his genius, by doing honest work for less than the usual Hollywood salary, by living in a cubbyhole where he had few visitors, and by staying away from parties. His only extravagance, except for buying conservative clothes, was a riding mare. Once the novelist Stephen Longstreet, then working in the same studio, found him sitting in a car at the curb, with the mare, swollen-bellied, behind him in a trailer.

"Hi, Bill, where you going?" Longstreet asked him.

Faulkner answered, "Home to Oxford. I don't want any mare of mine to throw a foal in California."

Faulkner himself was used to foaling his books in Oxford, but meanwhile the struggle against the Hollywood atmosphere must have been harder than he later made it appear. There is a note of triumph against odds in the letter that he sent me with the Compson genealogy: ". . . it took me about a week to get Hollywood out of my lungs, but I am still writing all right, I believe. . . . Maybe I am just happy that that damned west coast place has not cheapened my soul as much as I probably believed it was going to do."

But the problem of keeping alive his genius was still with him when he got back to Oxford; in fact it was becoming more difficult than ever. As his reputation spread, even the townspeople learned that he was a famous man, and some of them must have tried to invade his private life in the hope of being strengthened by his mana. There were also marauders from the outer world: "Last month two damned swedes, two days ago a confounded Chicago reporter, and now this one that cant even speak english. . . . I swear to christ being in hollywood was better than this where nobody knew me or cared a damn." He was faced with the beginning of the process by which an author is snatched from his private world and transformed into a public institution, a combined lecture hall, post office, and comfort station, all humming with strange voices and all surmounted with the effigy of the author as he had been.

Even at this early stage it must have been hard for him to maintain that "inner hush," as Fitzgerald calls it, in which the voices of his genius could be heard; there were always interruptions. One thinks of Coleridge and the dream he had that was "Kubla Khan." "On awaking," Coleridge said, speaking of the experience in the third person, "he appeared to himself to have a distinct recollection of the whole, and taking his pen, ink, and paper, instantly and eagerly wrote down the lines that are here preserved. At this moment he was unfortunately called out by a person on business from Porlock, and detained by him above an hour . . ." and that was the end of the vision. When Coleridge went back to his writing table, the rest of the poem "had passed away like the images on the surface of a stream into which a stone has been cast." Faulkner did not dream his stories (nor did Coleridge dream his poems, except for "Kubla Khan"). We shall never know how the stories first occurred to Faulkner, though it may be that the germ of more than one was the sort of "mental picture" that he mentioned as the beginning of *The Sound and the Fury*. It seems more certain, however, that they were consciously elaborated and revised in his mind, so that sometimes the process of setting them down was as simple as copying out a manuscript. At such times he could be interrupted by persons on business without damage to the text. The periods of solitude he required were the moments or hours when his imagination was at work and when intruders from Porlock might be fatal.

He stood at his threshold, as it were, to bar them out. He took measures against them, of which the simplest was not reading their letters, while in cases of threatened incursion he might flee to a cabin in the woods. Other measures failing, he was known to retreat behind an impenetrable wall of drunkenness; that too was in part a measure of self-protection. The intruders he feared were not the plain people of the town and countryside: hunters, carpenters, small farmers, black or white tenants, bootleggers, and deputy sheriffs; these offered no menace to his kingdom, and indeed they served to enrich its resources by the stories they told around campfires or sitting on the gallery of a crossroads store. There were many other people he was glad to see, for it is to be noted that one of his aims—besides that of protecting his imagined world—was living in the real world as a private person closely attached to family and friends. He was on cordial terms with his publishers and liked to work at Random House or at the Princeton residence of Saxe Commins. But that sort of private and professional life, with a degree of freedom and with days to be spent alone, could be preserved only by building walls against the world.

The strangers he feared were the infiltrators who tried to climb over or skirt around the walls—the correspondents, interviewers, would-be disciples, aspiring novelists, professors, literary ladies, and society people (unless they knew a lot about horses, in which case he enjoyed their company)—generally speaking, all those who were trying to use him or to make him over in their images. Sometimes he was rude to the wrong persons; I think of Ilya Ehrenburg, whom he would have found stimulating if they could have established communication, and there were many others. But the gifted people he snubbed might remember that, for all their gifts and good intentions, the part they might have played in Faulkner's days was that of persons from Porlock.

And Faulkner himself: did he find the right answers to his problems in life and in the continued production of his works? There are no completely right answers. It had better be said that his later books, in general, had not the freshness and power of the early ones. That is the common fate of imaginative writers (except for a few poets); some original force goes out of them. The books they write after the age of fifty most often lose in genius what they may possibly gain in talent. Faulkner lost substantially less than others did. Though none of his later books was on a level with *The Sound and the Fury* or *Go Down, Moses,* none of them made concessions to other people's tastes. One hears a person speaking in each of them, not an institution, and a person with reserves of power who may surprise us on any page. Some of Faulkner's best writing is in passages of *Requiem for a Nun* and *Intruder in the Dust* and especially—almost at the end—in the Mink Snopes chapters of *The Mansion.* In retrospect I should judge that he solved the problem of keeping alive his genius better than any other American novelist of our century.

Faulkner died almost exactly a year after Hemingway, eight months after James Thurber, and a few weeks before E. E. Cummings. Those were all great losses and, with earlier ones, they completely changed the literary landscape.

I think of their generation, which is also mine, as it started out many years ago. It was a generation like any other, I suppose, but it included what seems to be an extraordinary assortment of literary personalities. Of course the truth may be that the personalities, which might exist in any generation—which probably do exist there, by the law of averages—were given an extraordinary freedom to develop by the circumstances of the time. We started to publish in the postwar years, when our youth in itself was a moral asset. People seemed to feel that an older generation had let the world go to ruin, and they hoped that a new one might redeem it. The public was as grandly hospitable to young writers as it was to young movie actors and young financiers. Scott Fitzgerald was a best-selling novelist at twenty-four, and Glenway Wescott at twenty-seven. Hemingway, Dos Passos, Wilder, and Wolfe were all international figures at thirty. Even Faulkner, though slower to be recognized than the others, was a famous author in France while he was being neglected at home.

The generation had, like any other, a particular sense of life, which it was determined to express in books. Perhaps it felt more confidence than other generations have felt in its ability to make the books completely new. Everything in American literature seemed to be starting afresh. Every possibility seemed to be opening for the first time (since in those days we were splendidly ignorant of the American literary past), and almost any achievement seemed feasible. "I want to be one of the greatest writers who have ever lived, don't you?" Fitzgerald said to Edmund Wilson not long after they got out of Princeton. Wilson thought the remark was rather foolish, but he shared some of the feeling that lay behind it, as obviously Hemingway and Faulkner did. They all had a sense of being measured against the European past—against the future too—and of being called upon to do not only their best but something mysteriously better that could be done "without tricks and without cheating," as Hemingway said, if a writer was serious enough and had luck on his side.

Fortunate in the beginning, the generation was fortunate again after World War II. Most of the new writers who appeared in the 1950s were less adventurous than their predecessors had been in the realm of imaginative art, perhaps because their critical sense was more exacting and inhibiting.

They were given to writing critical studies, and the subject of these, in many cases, was the books that Faulkner and other famous men of his time had written twenty or thirty years before. Thus, in middle age the generation had the privilege of basking in a warm critical afterglow. Even its less prominent members acquired a sense of reassurance from the presence of their great contemporaries. Their world was like a forest in which the smaller trees were overshadowed and yet in some measure protected by the giants.

Then came the autumn gales, and most of the tallest trees were among the first to be uprooted.

Now, from where the forest stood, we seem to look out at a different landscape. There are no broad fields like those where we ran barefoot, no briary fencerows for quail to shelter in, and no green line on the horizon like that which used to mark the edge of the big woods. Everywhere in the flatland, the best farming country, are chickencoop houses in rows, in squares and circles, each house with its carport, its TV antenna, and its lady's green cambric handkerchief of lawn. An immense concrete freeway gouges through the hills and soars on high embankments over the streams, now poisoned, where we fished for trout. It is lined equidistantly with toy-sized cars, all drawn by hidden wires to the shopping center, where they stand in equidistant rows. From a hillside we watch their passengers go streaming into the supermarket, not one by one, but cluster by tight cluster, and we wonder whether they are speaking in a strange language. There must be giants among them, but distance makes them all look smaller than the men and women we knew.

Among the great dead, I find myself thinking of Faulkner with more affection than of others I also admired and knew more intimately. Perhaps it is owing to his peculiar mixture of genius and talent, of dignity and impishness, with a fairy-book innocence of mind. Though almost lacking in vanity —except in such minor concerns as riding jackets—he was the proudest man I knew. The pride made him act by his own standards, which were always difficult ones. In his Nobel Prize address, when he spoke of work accomplished "in the agony and sweat of the human spirit," he had reason to think of his own work. When he invoked "the courage and honor and hope and pride and compassion and pity and sacrifice" that have been the glory of man's past, his big words precisely named the qualities that he demanded of himself and that he achieved more often than the rest of us did, if always in his own fashion.

Sherman, Connecticut,
March 1966.

LIST OF LETTERS AND COMMENTARIES

INDEX

LIST OF LETTERS AND COMMENTARIES